# Contents

# Preface

A photograph in a city newspaper showed how a single incident could affect people in different ways. The picture showed two men sitting on a grassy knoll, listening to an unseen speaker. One of the men had tears trailing from the corners of his eyes down to a black beard that completely hid the lower portion of his face. He held a tiny American flag on a small stick in his right hand. The other man, half-turned away from the speaker, looked bored as he chewed upon a blade of grass. What brought tears to one man brought boredom to another.

For many Christians, a study of the New Testament might receive the same reception. For some, it brings the excitement of new and deeper discoveries about Jesus and his message; for others, it brings boredom! Today, however, the study of Scripture (and especially the New Testament) is becoming more popular and important to many people.

The Benziger New Testament Study Series joins a long line of study series on the New Testament. Like the others, it has a specific audience in mind, and in this way it differs from many others. This study is directed to those people who sit on grassy knolls, push baby carriages, rush off to work or school, play ball, dance, worry about family finances, crawl on the floor with babies, return home tired from work, and in general, to those who face all the tragic, joyful, and ordinary events of daily life. In short, the series is directed to people who live hectic, busy lives and who do not wish to rush home to a night of heavy reading.

This series aims to present a basic study of the New Testament in simple, nontechnical terms that will enable the readers to get a firm foundation for future study if they wish to continue to deepen their understanding of the New Testament. The readers who complete this study will have a good, basic understanding of the New Testament. This series is presented as a tool for those wishing to develop a love and understanding of the New Testament.

The Book of Revelation has always been a book of mystery and intrigue for many, and it has been interpreted as a book of doom for those who like to see in it predictions of the imminent end of the world. Preachers, at least in the past few centuries, have used the Book of Revelation as a means of showing that the signs of the end are all around us. The book has a far deeper meaning for the Christian caught in the midst of persecution. It is this meaning that we must understand and apply to our lives today. This volume is meant to help in that direction.

I would like to thank all those who have helped in the preparation of this work. I would like to thank Father Paul Wharton, a parish priest of the

Diocese of Wheeling-Charleston, who gave some very valuable insights into the development of the text. I would also like to thank Sister Anne Francis Bartus, SSJ, for her many corrections, Sister Mary Grace Freeman, SSJ and Sister Mary Immaculate Spires, SSJ, for the structural corrections they brought to this series. A special word of thanks goes also to Sister Anne Frances Lynch, VHM, for her many hours spent typing this manuscript. A final word of thanks goes to the parishioners of Saint Brendan parish in Elkins, West Virginia, who have made use of this series in an adult discussion program and to those permanent deacons in the Diocese of Wheeling-Charleston who have made use of an earlier draft of this series. I thank them all for their interest and suggestions.

# 1
# Background

During the Korean War, a radio operator behind enemy lines received a coded message ordering him to meet a small boat at a nearby beach. The message warned that the enemy was nearing his vicinity and that he had less than three hours to destroy his radio and to escape. Although the message was sent in code, the radio operator realized that the enemy would intercept the message, decipher the code and know exactly where he was to meet his boat. His hope and (he guessed) the hope of the one who sent the message was that it would take the enemy several hours to decipher the code, thus giving him time to get away. As it turned out, he escaped without incident, possibly while the enemy was still developing the code.

People in history have always made use of coded messages. When parents do not wish their children to know what they are saying, they often code their message by spelling out their words. Children use codes in games, thinking that adults are not able to understand their secret messages. Students in school use a type of code when they give nicknames to teachers, or when they speak with newly coined words that are meaningless to adults. Coded messages enable communication to take place in the unsuspecting presence of the one being spoken about. The Book of Revelation was written in the Roman Empire to encourage Christians to stand firm against Roman oppression. For the book to be circulated in the presence of the Romans, it had to be written in coded language. Our task is to decipher the code and to learn how its message applies to our world today.

## The Themes of Apocalyptic Literature

Throughout history, people have encountered events in their lives that seem to threaten the very roots of their faith and to prove that the power of evil easily conquers those who wish to follow the call of God. In the midst of such situations, apocalyptic writings came into being, which consist of secret "revelations," given to a certain saintly prophet who would remind the people that the present power of evil would eventually be overcome by good. Apocalyptic writings offer hope to people caught in the firm grip of evil powers.

The word *apocalypse* sounds like the Greek word "apocalypsis" from which it comes. The actual meaning of the word is "revelation." Religious apocalyptic writing consists of an uncovering, or a revelation, given by

God to offer the faithful hope for the future. Apocalyptic writings reveal that the present situation will soon end, that God, at the moment of destruction of the powers of evil, will save those who remain faithful, and that the just will share in a new and glorious life. In apocalyptic writings, the author indicates signs that will show the end of the present situation is about to occur. Apocalyptic writings are filled with highly symbolic images that speak of catastrophes taking place in the heavens and on earth. There will be war and earthquakes; the heavenly bodies (sun, moon, and stars) will fall from their place in the skies, and a visitation from God will take place. These symbols and others used in apocalyptic writings are taken from ancient myths, beliefs about world structure, poetry, prophecy, history, and other forms of literature.

The authors of apocalyptic writings often choose the name of a well-known authority from the past who speaks as if he were foretelling the events from his own viewpoint in time. The Book of Daniel is an example of this. Daniel was a Jew who lived in Babylon in the early sixth century before Christ. The Book of Daniel, however, was not written until the middle of the second century before Christ. The author uses Daniel, who lived four centuries earlier, to foretell what was to happen to Israel in the second century before Christ. Since the one actually writing the book is living through the events described, he is able to report them with accuracy.

Apocalyptic writings are also concerned with teachings about the end of time. The name given to these teachings about the end comes from several Greek words that form the term *eschaton*. The eschaton plays a central role in apocalyptic literature and usually concerns the glorious end in store for those who remain faithful. After the struggles of the present day are ended, God will triumph, and those who have remained faithful will enter an eternal paradise with God. This knowledge can only be gained through "revelation," since it predicts events beyond our human knowledge.

# The Book of Revelation as Apocalyptic Literature

Although the Book of Revelation has many of the features mentioned above, it differs in some ways from the Jewish apocalyptic literature found in the Old Testament. Instead of reaching into the past to choose the name of a prophetic authority, the writer of the Book of Revelation names himself (John) as the author of the book. As we shall see later, however, the author, true to apocalyptic form, appears to be living before the events he describes, although he is actually living through them.

Another difference found in the Book of Revelation is that it seems in part to follow a letter format. The book begins with letters to seven churches in Asia Minor. Such a letter format is completely foreign to apocalyptic literature, and may possibly have its origin in the high respect gained for the letters of Paul the Apostle. The format of letter writing, however, does not continue throughout the book.

The Book of Revelation has many features in common with apocalyptic literature: it speaks about the eschaton; it makes use of ancient symbols and images found in other apocalyptic writings; it uses prophetic writings, most notably the apocalyptic writings of Ezekiel and Daniel; it is written for people living during a time of persecution; it offers hope for the future; and its use of myth, symbol, and history, for example, enables its passage throughout the Roman Empire without the Roman officials' awareness of its content. In the Book of Revelation, the Roman Empire is known as "Babylon," the ancient empire that overran Judea six centuries before Christ and led many of its inhabitants into exile.

In reading the Book of Revelation and any apocalyptic work, we must keep in mind that the author had no intention of predicting events far into the future that would signal the end of the world for later generations. Instead, the authors were writing for their own day, and they referred to current events. To use the Book of Revelation in our world today as a book that foretold signs now occurring and signaling the end of the world is to miss the message of the book. It was a book of hope offered to people in a time of persecution, most notably the time during which the author was writing. It nevertheless has applications to other times in history and offers hope to others in time of persecution, but it does not intend to list a number of signs indicating that the world is about to end. Unfortunately, every century throughout history can count the many misuses of the Book of Revelation by those who preached (from the signs found in the Book) that the world was about to end. Even our own century is not free from those who would use the book in this manner.

## Occasion

The Roman Empire often revered their kings as gods, and they ordered that the people of the empire, even those in conquered territories, honor their kings in this way. According to the Roman mentality, this practice posed very few problems, since it did not mean denouncing one's gods, but simply adding another god to the list. The Romans believed in many gods, and the addition of the name of the emperor to the gods would cause little problem.

After they gained control of the Jewish nation, the Romans soon discovered that the Jewish people worshiped only one God, and they refused to add the name of another god to that of the one they called the true God. After a long and sometimes bloody struggle, Rome finally recognized the Jewish faith as an official religion of the empire, and they excused the Jews from adding the name of the emperor to their worship of God.

When Jesus' followers were cast out of Jewish circles and as they began to reject some of the traditions of Judaism, Rome refused to identify them with Judaism, and Christians found themselves no longer exempt from emperor worship. In some areas, persecutions were taking place against Christians who refused to worship the emperor as a god. The author of the Book of Revelation writes for those who are undergoing such a persecution. Although the persecution may not have been widespread at the time of the writing, it does seem to have been strong in the area where the book was being written. The author wanted to give those undergoing this persecution a reason for hope in a better future. He wanted to tell them that evil, although it seemed so powerful now, is only allowed to act as long as God wills it. The time of evil's power will soon come to an end.

## Author and Date

The author identifies himself as John who is writing from an island named Patmos. Patmos was used by the Roman officials as a place of exile for those whom they wished to punish. In the Book of Revelation, we learn that the author is exiled to the island of Patmos because he proclaimed the Word of God and gave witness to Jesus Christ (1:9).

Throughout history, many writers have identified the author of this book with John, the son of Zebedee. As early as the mid-second century, writers were referring to the author as Zebedee's son. Others believed that John, the son of Zebedee, was also responsible for all the New Testament letters attributed to John. The style, language, and imagery of the Book of Revelation differ so drastically from the Johannine writings that few agree with this idea. Some commentators, however, would say that it is more likely that John, the son of Zebedee, wrote the Book of Revelation than that he wrote any of the Johannine writings. Most commentators are in agreement that we do not know who wrote the Book of Revelation.

Most commentators, looking at the book itself, feel that John was a well-known teacher of the early Church and that he held some office of authority or was, at least, held in very high esteem. He speaks with authority and uses his own name in writing the letter. The use of his real name indicates that he was a person of some influence in early Christianity. He calls himself a "brother," thus indicating that he is a Christian, and most likely one who identifies with the Christians of Asia Minor. He also calls himself a "slave" of Jesus Christ, a title used by those who dedicated themselves to sharing Christ's message with others.

Most commentators believe that the book was written toward the end of the first century, during the reign of Domitian, a ruthless and brutal Roman ruler who died around A.D. 96. Many of the events described seem to point to events occurring during Domitian's reign. Domitian had statues of himself set up throughout the empire, and he nurtured the idea of emperor worship.

# Outline

*Prologue and Letters to the Seven Churches*    In this passage, the author presents the title of his book, and he addresses letters to seven churches in Asia Minor. Although he is writing to specific churches, the letters are really meant to be addresses to all churches.

*The Heavenly Vision and Seven Seals*    This section consists of visions of God enthroned in heaven, being worshiped by hosts of heaven and the angels. The lamb breaks open the seven seals, and each event is acted out to give its message.

*The Seven Trumpets*    In this section, the author lists the seven catastrophes that are unleashed with the opening of the seventh seal. Seven plagues are set free by seven trumpet blasts.

*The Unnumbered Visions*    These chapters offer a sequence of unnumbered visions that speak of war between good and evil and the eventual conquest by good.

*The Seven Bowls*    These are the seven bowls of God's wrath that will be poured out on those who follow the dragon and who wear the mark of the beast. The sinfulness of Babylon leads to God's wrath and the fall of Babylon. The heavenly hosts rejoice in the fall of this empire.

*Fulfilling God's Plan*    Christ comes, the last battle ensues, judgment follows, and a new heaven and a new earth begin.

# Review

1. What is apocalyptic literature?
2. How does the Book of Revelation fit into apocalyptic literature?
3. What is the occasion for the writing of the Book of Revelation?
4. Who is the author of the Book of Revelation and when was it written?
5. Give a short outline of the Book of Revelation.

# For Further Reflection

1. Many people today see the Book of Revelation as a book that predicts the signs of the end of the world. If this is not the case, then what value does the Book of Revelation have for our own day?
2. Do we have any types of writings today that are parallel to apocalyptic writing?

# 2
# Prologue and Letters to the Seven Churches

Rv 1: 1–3

**1** ¹**The revelation of Jesus Christ, which God gave to him, to show his servants what must happen soon. He made it known by sending his angel to his servant John, ²who gives witness to the word of God and to the testimony of Jesus Christ by reporting what he saw. ³Blessed is the one who reads aloud and blessed are those who listen to this prophetic message and heed what is written in it, for the appointed time is near.**

Many commentators believe that the prologue of the Book of Revelation is actually the title of the book. The author begins by speaking of a revelation, a mystery unveiled by God that speaks of those things soon to occur. True to apocalyptic form, the author presents God as a distant God, concerned but far removed in the divine realm of heaven. God passes the revelation on to Jesus Christ, who, in turn, passes it on to John through an angel. This angel is Christ's special angel and is called by the author "his angel."

John's ministry involves the sharing of this revelation with all Christians, whom the author calls "his (Christ's) servants." John sees himself as a living witness to the Word of God and the testimony of Jesus Christ, that is, he witnesses with his life to the revelation he is sharing. The term "witness" can refer to one who is a martyr for the faith, or to one who suffers hardship for the faith. John admits that he is undergoing hardship for his proclamation of the faith (1:9). As a living witness of God's message, John is also a living witness to the death and resurrection of Jesus. Jesus' death and resurrection is the witness that comes from Christ himself, reflected by John in his own witnessing.

The author of Revelation gives the first of seven beatitudes by proclaiming that those who read, hear, and respond to what is written are called blessed, or spiritually happy. The number seven—a sacred, symbolic number that means fullness or completion— is used often throughout the book. The beatitudes reflect the fullness of the heavenly gifts. The author presumes that his message will be read aloud in the assembly and that those who hear it and live it will receive God's blessings. Although the author calls his message a "prophetic message," it should actually be considered an apocalyptic message, since it has all the elements of apocalypse. To the prophet, God is near, speaking through him or her, while the apocalyptic witness sees God as distant, passing the message on through other messengers along the way. The prologue ends with the typical apocalyptic urgency: ". . . the time is near."

**Rv 1:
4–8**

*Greeting*     **⁴John, to the seven churches in Asia: grace to you and peace from him who is and who was and who is to come, and from the seven spirits before his throne, ⁵and from Jesus Christ, the faithful witness, the firstborn of the dead and ruler of the kings of the earth. To him who loves us and has freed us from our sins by his blood, ⁶who has made us into a kingdom, priests for his God and Father, to him be glory and power forever [and ever]. Amen.**

> **⁷Behold, he is coming amid the clouds,**
>    **and every eye will see him,**
>       **even those who pierced him.**
> **All the peoples of the earth will lament him.**
>       **Yes. Amen.**

**⁸"I am the Alpha and the Omega," says the Lord God, "the one who is and who was and who is to come, the almighty."**

John begins a general introduction to the seven letters to follow, and he uses the customary greeting found in Christians' letters of the early Church. He identifies those to whom he is writing, names himself as the writer, and wishes them grace and peace. Although he addresses his letter to the churches in Asia Minor, most commentators believe that he is addressing all churches. The number seven implies completeness or fullness, and, in this case, it points to the whole Church. The names of the churches that will follow are all significant communities along a commonly used trade route.

John speaks as a witness to God "who is, who was, and who is to come." God is an active and concerned God. John also passes on greetings from the "seven spirits before his throne." Most commentators believe that this refers to the seven archangels whom later Jewish writers saw as holding a special place before God. He finally sends greetings from Jesus Christ who is the faithful witness through his life, death, and resurrection. Jesus is also called the firstborn from the dead, which is a reference to his resurrection, and the ruler of the kings of the earth, which places him above all earthly authority. John is already implying that emperor worship ignores the superiority of Jesus Christ over Roman rulers.

Apocalyptic writings abound with hymns of praise. John praises Jesus Christ for his love, for the salvation he brought us through his death and resurrection, and for the gift of making us priests in the service of God. The author offers eternal praise and power to Jesus Christ.

The passage concerning the general introduction to the letters ends with prophetic proclamations from some Old Testament prophets. The author of the Book of Daniel writes that he saw the One, "like the son of man," coming on the clouds of heaven (7:13). John calls his readers to behold the one—who he implies is Jesus Christ—coming on the clouds of heaven. He makes use of a quotation from the prophet Zechariah who speaks of looking on the one who is thrust through (12:10), and he tells his readers that all shall see Christ, even those who pierced him. John pictures the whole world in mourning over Jesus. This is the testimony of Jesus as found in his life, death, resurrection, and glorification.

John makes use of the first letter of the Greek alphabet (alpha) and the last letter (omega) to show that God is the beginning and end of all. Although he applies this symbol to God the Father, John also uses it to refer to Jesus Christ. John again speaks of God as the One who is, who was, and who is to come. He adds that God is the "Almighty," a reference to God's divinity.

| | |
|---|---|
| **Rv 1: 9–20** | ***The First Vision***    ⁹I, John, your brother, who share with you the distress, the kingdom, and the endurance we have in Jesus, found myself on the island called Patmos because I proclaimed God's word and gave testimony to Jesus. ¹⁰I was caught up in spirit on the Lord's day and heard behind me a voice as loud as a trumpet, ¹¹which said, "Write on a scroll what you see and send it to the seven churches: to Ephesus, Smyrna, Pergamum, Thyatira, Sardis, Philadelphia, and Laodicea." ¹²Then I turned to see whose voice it was that spoke to me, and when I turned, I saw seven gold lampstands ¹³and in the midst of the lampstands one like a son of man, wearing an ankle-length robe, with a gold sash around his chest. ¹⁴The hair of his head was as white as white wool or as snow, and his eyes were like a fiery flame. ¹⁵His feet were like polished brass refined in a furnace, and his voice was like the sound of rushing water. |

<sup>16</sup>In his right hand he held seven stars. A sharp two-edged sword came out of his mouth, and his face shone like the sun at its brightest.

<sup>17</sup>When I caught sight of him, I fell down at his feet as though dead. He touched me with his right hand and said, "Do not be afraid. I am the first and the last, <sup>18</sup>the one who lives. Once I was dead, but now I am alive forever and ever. I hold the keys to death and the netherworld. <sup>19</sup>Write down, therefore, what you have seen, and what is happening, and what will happen afterwards. <sup>20</sup>This is the secret meaning of the seven stars you saw in my right hand, and of the seven gold lampstands: the seven stars are the angels of the seven churches, and the seven lampstands are the seven churches.

John expresses his condition as a witness. He is living in exile on the island of Patmos because of his proclamation of the Word of God and the witness he bore for Jesus Christ. Like his readers, John is undergoing hardship, knowing that the true reign is not that of worldly emperors, but that of Jesus Christ. He shares in their endurance in the faith which enables them to bear all for the sake of the faith.

John's vision begins on the "Lord's Day," which is Sunday, the first day of the week. The sacred day for the Jewish people is Saturday, the last day of the week which they call the Sabbath. The sacred feast day for Christians is Sunday, the first day of the week and the day on which Christ was raised from the dead. On this sacred day, John experienced a vision in which he heard a piercing voice, like the sound of a trumpet, instructing him to write down his experience. The voice of God comes to the prophets of the Old Testament, sounding like a trumpet blast (Ez 3:12).

During the vision, John is instructed to write down what he sees and hears and to send it to the seven churches. The message does not come from John to the churches, but from Christ. John is simply the intermediary for the message. He is told to write to Ephesus, Smyrna, Pergamum, Thyatira, Sardis, Philadelphia, and Laodicea. As already mentioned, these churches are along a trade route and represent all churches.

When John turns to see who has spoken, he sees seven lampstands representing the seven churches. Using an expression from the Book of Daniel, he tells us that he sees ". . . One like a Son of Man" (Dn 7:13) standing in the midst of the lampstands. The picture is one of Jesus who looks human, but who is also a heavenly being, in the image of God. Borrowing again from Old Testament images, John tells us that he had a sash of gold and an ankle-length robe, a picture of an angelic being found in the Book of Daniel (10:5). In the same prophetic book, we read that the Ancient One took his throne, wearing snow bright clothing and having hair that was white as wool (Dn 7:9–10). His eyes were like fiery torches, his feet and arms like shining bronze, and his voice like the roar of a large crowd (Dn 10:6). John applies all of these images to the One who was like a Son of Man.

Jesus held seven stars in his right hand. In ancient times, the emperor was pictured as holding seven stars in his hand as a representation of his authority. By picturing Jesus as having seven stars in his hands, the author is telling us that Jesus is the true ruler of the universe. From his mouth comes a sharp two-edged sword, a symbol from the Old Testament referring to the Word of God (see Is 11:4, 49:2; Wis 18:15). Jesus' face, like that of God, shone brighter than the brightest sun.

In reading this section, we should not attempt to put together a visual picture similar to that of the author, since he is not giving us a portrait of Jesus but is sharing a message about Jesus.

In many visions in the Old Testament, those who found themselves in God's presence often reacted with fear and fell prostrate before such a vision (Gn 32:31; Dn 8:18, 10:9–11; Wis 18:15). John falls prostrate before this great vision, and Jesus touches him, telling him not to fear. Jesus now accepts for himself images that properly belong to God. He calls himself the First and the Last, and the One who lives. Through his resurrection, Jesus has been raised from the dead to live forever, holding in his hands the keys of death and the place of the dead. Through the symbol of the keys, Jesus has now mastered death.

Jesus tells John to write down what he sees now and what he will see in the future. He then tells John the secret of the seven stars and the seven lampstands. According to Jesus, the stars represent the seven spirits of the seven churches. Most commentators believe that the seven spirits refer to the guardian angels depicted throughout Jewish thought. The fact that Jesus holds the seven stars in his hands points to his authority not only over the universe but also over the churches who will soon receive his message. The seven lampstands, as we have already learned, represent these seven churches.

|  |  |
|---|---|
| **Rv 2:**<br>**1–7** | **2**    *To Ephesus*    [1]"To the angel of the church in Ephesus, write this:<br>        " 'The one who holds the seven stars in his right hand and walks in the midst of the seven gold lampstands says |

this: <sup>2</sup>"I know your works, your labor, and your endur-ance, and that you cannot tolerate the wicked; you have tested those who call themselves apostles but are not, and discovered that they are impostors. <sup>3</sup>Moreover, you have endurance and have suffered for my name, and you have not grown weary. <sup>4</sup>Yet I hold this against you: you have lost the love you had at first. <sup>5</sup>Realize how far you have fallen. Repent, and do the works you did at first. Other-wise, I will come to you and remove your lampstand from its place, unless you repent. <sup>6</sup>But you have this in your favor: you hate the works of the Nicolaitans, which I also hate.

<sup>7</sup>" ' "Whoever has ears ought to hear what the Spirit says to the churches. To the victor I will give the right to eat from the tree of life that is in the garden of God." ' "

John is ordered to write the first of his seven letters to the angel of the Church at Ephesus. Although he is told to write to the guardian angel of the Church, he is actually ordered to write to the Church community. Because of the importance of the city of Ephesus at the time of John, the Church there is also considered important. Paul the Apostle spent more time at Ephesus than at any other place during his missionary journeys. The Roman Empire considered Ephesus to be an important city for trade, and it had received much support from Rome. If emperor worship were to survive anywhere in the empire, it would be at Ephesus. The importance of the city as well as its loyalty to Rome may likely have prompted John to address his first letter to this city.

The letter is presented as coming from Christ, the One who walks among the lampstands. Christ first praises the community at Ephesus for their good deeds and for their endurance in the faith: they have refused to bear with evil men who falsely call themselves apostles, and they have not become impatient or discouraged in the face of hardships. The com-munity's faithfulness is especially noteworthy since Christians who lived in a city so devoted to Rome could have been persecuted for not worship-ing the emperor.

Christ, however, finds fault with them for turning away from their first love, that is, their early fervor in the faith. Although he does not specify exactly what they have done in turning away from their first love, he does call them back to their former deeds. Because they had such a firm faith in the beginning, they have fallen far, and Christ threatens to remove their lampstand from its place unless they repent. Christ's warning may signify that the Church at Ephesus will lose its high place in the early Church, or that it will be completely abandoned.

Christ returns to praising the Church at Ephesus as he compliments them on their stand against a heretical group, known as the Nicolaitans. In this first letter, we are told nothing about the teachings of this false group, but they will be mentioned again in the third letter.

The first letter ends (as all of them do) with a call to the community to heed what the Spirit is saying to the Churches. Christ promises that those who remain faithful will eat from the tree of life which grows in God's garden. This is a reference to the garden of Eden and the events which took place there. Instead of losing paradise, the faithful Christian will share in God's eternal garden of paradise and will eat of the fruit of the tree of life.

|  |  |
|---|---|
| **Rv 2:** **8–11** | *To Smyrna*    **8"To the angel of the church in Smyrna, write this:** |
|  | **" 'The first and the last, who once died but came to life, says this: 9"I know your tribulation and poverty, but you are rich. I know the slander of those who claim to be Jews and are not, but rather are members of the assembly of Satan. 10Do not be afraid of anything that you are going to suffer. Indeed, the devil will throw some of you into prison, that you may be tested, and you will face an ordeal for ten days. Remain faithful until death, and I will give you the crown of life.** |
|  | **11" ' "Whoever has ears ought to hear what the Spirit says to the churches. The victor shall not be harmed by the second death." ' "** |

The second letter is written to Smyrna, another important commercial city located just north of Ephesus. In each of these letters, Christ is revealed by means of one of the several images presented in the first chapter of this book (1:12–19). In the letter to the Church at Ephesus, John used the image of Christ as the One who holds the seven stars in his hand and walks among the seven lampstands, thereby showing Christ's authority over the destiny of the Churches. In this second letter, the image chosen represents Christ as the First and the Last, the one who once died but now lives (1:17–18). In the letter to Smyrna, John speaks of conflict and the apparent power of evil. Christ, as the First and the Last, will nevertheless conquer, and the one who once died, but now lives, will bring the faithful to a new life.

In each of these visions, Christ tells the Churches that he knows of their situation. In this case, he tells the community of Smyrna that he is familiar with their hardships and their poverty in the midst of riches. This poverty may be an allusion to the spiritual poverty of the area, or the fact that Christians were not being hired because of their beliefs. Christ tells them that he knows of the afflictions they suffer at the hands of those who claim to be Jews, but who in reality are not. Since there were many Jews living in Smyrna, John may be referring to those who have rejected Christ, or to those who have faith in Christ, but who live as if they are Jews in order to avoid persecution. In reality, those causing this hardship are not faithful Jews. John does not intend to express any anti-Semitism in this passage.

Those who remain faithful to Christ have no need for fear. Although they might be cast into prison by agents of the devil, they will eventually receive the crown of life. This crown of life likely refers to the crown of victory that was presented at Greek athletic events, or it may have had its origin in Old Testament texts. Its meaning, however, is clear. The crown of life—eternal reward—is promised to those who persevere. Christ tells them that they will face this affliction for a period of ten days, a symbolic number meaning that the days of the devil's power are limited. Such a reference, however, should not be taken literally as exactly ten days.

Christ has John conclude this letter to Ephesus, as he does the others, by calling on his listeners to heed his words, to put them into action. Those who are faithful will not face a "second death" by facing eternal punishment after their physical death.

---

**Rv 2: 12–17**

*To Pergamum*  ¹²"To the angel of the church in Pergamum, write this:

" 'The one with the sharp two-edged sword says this: ¹³"I know that you live where Satan's throne is, and yet you hold fast to my name and have not denied your faith in me, not even in the days of Antipas, my faithful witness, who was martyred among you, where Satan lives. ¹⁴Yet I have a few things against you. You have some people there who hold to the teaching of Balaam, who instructed Balak to put a stumbling block before the Israelites: to eat food sacrificed to idols and to play the harlot. ¹⁵Likewise, you also have some people who hold to the teaching of [the] Nicolaitans. [16]Therefore, repent. Otherwise, I will come to you quickly and wage war against them with the sword of my mouth.

[17]" ' "Whoever has ears ought to hear what the Spirit says to the churches. To the victor I shall give some of the hidden manna; I shall also give a white amulet upon which is inscribed a new name, which no one knows except the one who receives it." ' "

The third letter is sent to the Church at Pergamum, the city where Rome established its seat of government in Asia. The author calls the city the place where the "throne of Satan" is erected, a reference to its political position within the empire. The letter recalls the symbol of the two-edged sword used for Christ in the first chapter (1:16), and its meaning is one of judgment. The Christians of this town held firm in the faith, even when one of their number, Antipas, was killed for not rejecting it.

After these words of praise, Pergamum, like the other cities, receives a warning. In the Book of Numbers, we read that Balak, the king of the Moabites, sends for Balaam to have him curse the Israelite nation. Although the Lord does not permit Balaam to curse the Israelites, they eventually commit sin by having illicit relations with the Moabite women and by eating the food sacrificed to idols (Nm 23:1–25:5). Christ tells the people of Pergamum that they are like the Israelites of old when they follow the teaching of the Nicolaitans. The Nicolaitans apparently taught that Christians could honor the emperor as a god, since such a god did not actually exist, and that they could eat the food offered to nonexistent and false idols. The Lord warns his listeners that if they do not repent, he will come and fight them with the sword of his mouth, that is, he will pass a harsh judgment on them. The Israelites of old were executed for their sins, and the implication is that Christians will share in a spiritual execution, by being cut off from God.

Christ calls the church at Pergamum (as he calls the others) to hear his words and put them into action. Instead of eating food offered to idols, they will share in eternal victory by taking part in the hidden manna (the Eucharist). In the days when John was writing his book, some people had the superstitious practice of having magical names, known only to themselves and used to ward off evil spirits. Christ, in opposition to this superstition, tells those who heed his word that they will have a new, hidden name inscribed on a white stone. This new name will be received at the time of their eternal victory.

*To Thyatira* [18]"To the angel of the church in Thyatira, write this:

" 'The Son of God, whose eyes are like a fiery flame and whose feet are like polished brass, says this: [19]"I know your works, your love, faith, service, and endurance, and that your last works are greater than the first. [20]Yet I hold this against you, that you tolerate the woman Jezebel, who calls herself a prophetess, who teaches and misleads my servants to play the harlot and to eat food sacrificed to idols. [21]I have given her time to repent, but she refuses to repent of her harlotry. [22]So I will cast her on a sickbed and plunge those who commit adultery with her into intense suffering unless they repent of her works. [23]I will also put her children to death. Thus shall all the churches come to know that I am the searcher of hearts and minds and that I will give each of you what your works deserve. [24]But I say to the rest of you in Thyatira, who do not uphold this teaching and know nothing of the so-called deep secrets of Satan; on you I will place no further burden, [25]except that you must hold fast to what you have until I come.

[26]" ' "To the victor, who keeps to my ways until the end,
I will give authority over the nations.
[27]He will rule them with an iron rod.
Like clay vessels will they be smashed,
[28]just as I received authority from my Father. And to him I will give the morning star.

[29]" 'Whoever has ears ought to hear what the Spirit says to the churches." ' "

The fourth letter is written to Thyatira, and Christ, the sender of the message, is here described as the one whose eyes blaze like fire and whose feet are like polished brass. This image, as the earlier images of Christ, is taken from the first chapter (1:14–15), and it symbolizes Christ as the one who sees into the depths of all and judges all. As in the previous letters, Christ proclaims what he knows of the Christians of Thyatira and he praises them for their virtues of love, faith, service and endurance. Endurance here refers to their courage in standing firm and not allowing themselves to be lured into idol worship. In recent times, they are apparently being harassed even more for their faith.

A warning, however, follows these words of praise. The author makes use of an image from Jezebel, a false Old Testament prophetess. Jezebel was the wife of King Ahab of Israel, and she worshiped the idol Baal (1 Kg 16:31). Christ tells the people of Thyatira that they are tolerating "a Jezebel" and are committing the same crimes of sexual sinfulness and eating food sacrificed to idols. The sins are the same as those identified with the Nicolaitans.

Christ has given this idolatrous woman an opportunity to repent, but she refused. As a result, she must suffer for her sinfulness, and those who sin with her will likewise suffer. Her children, meaning those who follow her ways, will face spiritual death. All the Churches who witness this outcome will recognize that Christ sees far into the minds and hearts of all and that he judges all as they deserve.

Different groups exist within the Thyatira community: those who have chosen to follow the ways of idol worship, and those who know nothing of these "deep secrets" of Satan. Christ addresses those who have remained faithful, declaring that they must remain faithful until he comes. They will then take part in the victory of Christ, sharing in the authority he has received from the Father. He shall have a rule as strong as a rod of iron, and those who sin shall shatter like crockery before him. Those who remain faithful will receive the morning star. They will share in the presence of Christ.

This letter to the Church at Thyatira ends with the usual call for all to heed what they have heard.

| | |
|---|---|
| **Rv 3: 1–6** | **3** *To Sardis* [1]"To the angel of the church in Sardis, write this:<br><br>" 'The one who has the seven spirits of God and the seven stars says this: "I know your works, that you have the reputation of being alive, but you are dead. [2]Be watchful and strengthen what is left, which is going to die, for I have not found your works complete in the sight of my God. [3]Remember then how you accepted and heard; keep it, and repent. If you are not watchful, I will come like a thief, and you will never know at what hour I will come upon you. [4]However, you have a few people in Sardis who have not soiled their garments; they will walk with me dressed in white, because they are worthy. |

⁵" 'The victor will thus be dressed in white, and I will never erase his name from the book of life but will acknowledge his name in the presence of my Father and of his angels.

⁶" 'Whoever has ears ought to hear what the Spirit says to the churches." ' "

The next letter is sent to the Church at Sardis, a city thirty miles southeast of Thyatira. The city was destroyed by an earthquake in 17 B.C. and was then rebuilt by the emperor Tiberius. In this letter, Christ is portrayed as the one who holds the seven spirits, that is, the seven stars, in his hand (1:4, 20). As the ruler of all the Churches, Christ speaks with authority and a warning for all. He tells the Church at Sardis that although to many their faith seems to be alive, it is, in reality, dead. Christ immediately softens this harsh statement by further urging that they should awaken and strengthen their faith, which is now on the verge of death. Their faith is not dead, Christ states, but unless they change their way of life, it soon will be dead.

Christ tells them that they are not living up to their call and the message they first received with enthusiasm. If they do not change, Christ warns that he will come to them like a thief in the night. This image is also found in the Gospel of Matthew (24:43), and it speaks of the suddenness of Christ's coming rather than the idea that Christ will be stealing a material possession. This idea of a sudden ending for the world is used often in apocalyptic writings.

In the city of Sardis, some have remained faithful by not soiling their garments. The imagery of garments—whether white or soiled—alludes to one's inner disposition and not literally to the clothing one is wearing. In the baptismal rite, those who were baptized come out of the water and put on a white robe to signify their inner dedication and purity. Christ declares that the ones who are faithful will be the ones clothed victoriously in white. Christ will witness to their faithfulness before the Father and his angels. The names of those who remain faithful will not be erased from the Book of Life. The image of the Book of Life, often mentioned later in the Book of Revelation, represents one's citizenship in eternal life. In becoming a Christian, a person becomes a citizen of this life, and only by rejecting faith will a person's name be erased from this book.

This letter to the Church at Sardis ends with Christ's customary call to heed his words.

**Rv 3:
7–13**

*To Philadelphia*     [7]"To the angel of the church in Philadelphia, write this:

> " 'The holy one, the true,
>> who holds the key of David,
>> who opens and no one shall close,
>> who closes and no one shall open,

says this:

[8]" ' "I know your works (behold, I have left an open door before you, which no one can close). You have limited strength, and yet you have kept my word and have not denied my name. [9]Behold, I will make those of the assembly of Satan who claim to be Jews and are not, but are lying, behold I will make them come and fall prostrate at your feet, and they will realize that I love you. [10]Because you have kept my message of endurance, I will keep you safe in the time of trial that is going to come to the whole world to test the inhabitants of the earth. [11]I am coming quickly. Hold fast to what you have, so that no one may take your crown.

[12]" ' "The victor I will make into a pillar in the temple of my God, and he will never leave it again. On him I will inscribe the name of my God and the name of the city of my God, the new Jerusalem, which comes down out of heaven from my God, as well as my new name.

[13]" 'Whoever has ears ought to hear what the Spirit says to the churches." ' "

Christ tells John to write his sixth letter to Philadelphia, a city southeast of Sardis. Christ is here portrayed as the holy and true One, references that recall the same words of praise given to God in the Old Testament (Is 6:3; 40:25). He has the power of the keys of David, a reference to Christ as the true successor of David. Isaiah relays a story of someone receiving the key of the house of David which gives him the right to open what no one shall shut, and to shut what no one shall open (Is 22:22). The Scriptures often use the image of keys to signify power.

Christ has high words of praise for the Church at Philadelphia. He knows of their good deeds and thus opens a door for them that no one can shut. This door may further signify the opportunity to suffer for Christ or, more likely, the door of eternal life. Despite their small size and political weakness, the Church at Philadelphia is withstanding the persecution of the self-proclaimed Jews whom Christ sees as frauds. The true Jews are those who accept Christ as the fulfillment of the Old Testament prophecies. Christ calls these false Jews, who have turned away from him, "Satan's assembly," a title that indicates their rejection of the true faith. In the Book of Isaiah, the prophet pictures great nations as falling prostrate before those who have God with them (45:14). The Jews who do not recognize Christ will join this long line of pagans from the Old Testament and will likewise fall prostrate before the true followers of God. Because the Church at Philadelphia has held firm to Christ's message, they will not undergo the afflictions of the pagans who have made the world their dwelling place.

Christ tells his readers that he is coming soon, urging them to remain strong and not to lose the crown of eternal life they have received. As victors, they shall be like pillars in the new heavenly temple. They will bear the marks of the elect—the name of God, the name of the New Jerusalem, and the new and glorified name of Jesus Christ.

The letter ends with the usual call to heed these words.

**Rv 3: 14–22**

**To Laodicea**  **[14]"To the angel of the church in Laodicea, write this:**

**" 'The Amen, the faithful and true witness, the source of God's creation, says this: [15]"I know your works; I know that you are neither cold nor hot. I wish you were either cold or hot. [16]So, because you are lukewarm, neither hot nor cold, I will spit you out of my mouth. [17]For you say, 'I am rich and affluent and have no need of anything,' and yet do not realize that you are wretched, pitiable, poor, blind, and naked. [18]I advise you to buy from me gold refined by fire so that you may be rich, and white garments to put on so that your shameful nakedness may not be exposed, and buy ointment to smear on your eyes so that you may see. [19]Those whom I love, I reprove and chastise. Be earnest, therefore, and repent.**

**[20]" ' "Behold, I stand at the door and knock. If anyone hears my voice and opens the door, [then] I will enter his house and dine with him, and he with me. [21]I will give the victor the right to sit with me on my throne, as I myself first won the victory and sit with my Father on his throne.**

²²" ' "Whoever has ears ought to hear what the Spirit says to the churches." ' "

The final message goes to the Church at Laodicea, a city southeast of Philadelphia. In this letter, Christ is called the "Amen, the faithful and true witness," and "the source of God's creation." These images seem to refer to Christ's resurrection, which concludes the old age and begins a new age. In the first chapter, Christ is referred to as the "faithful and true witness" (1:5), traits found lacking in the Church at Laodicea.

When Christ expresses what he knows of this Church, he offers no praise, but instead accuses them of being complacent, neither hot nor cold, but only lukewarm and sickening enough to be vomited up. They are apparently enjoying great wealth and look with pity on the other Churches in the midst of suffering, thankful that they themselves are not undergoing such misfortunes. Christ tells them that they are deceiving themselves, since in reality they are miserable, poor, blind, and naked. He urges them to find true riches in gold refined by fire, which symbolizes the suffering involved in being a true witness to Christ. They should cover themselves with the white garments of dedication to Christ and anoint their eyes with the oil of spiritual understanding. Since these images point to suffering for Christ, Christ reminds them that chastisements and not riches are a true sign of their love. He calls the Church at Laodicea to a sincere change of life.

An image of the new age is often presented as the banquet of the Lord. A banquet also has the deeper meaning of inviting a person into one's life. Christ stands at the door and knocks, looking for the Church of Laodicea to open and invite him into their lives. When he does enter, he will share in the banquet of the new age with them. Those who are victorious by sharing their lives with Christ will also share in Christ's glory beside his Father's throne in glory.

This last letter to the Church at Laodicea concludes with the same words as the previous six letters, calling those who read Christ's words to bring them into their lives.

# Review

1. How does John describe Christ to his readers?
2. What are some significant points of John's letter to Ephesus?
3. What are some significant points of John's letter to Smyrna?
4. What are some significant points of John's letter to Pergamum?
5. What are some significant points of John's letter to Thyatira?

6. What are some significant points of John's letter to Sardis?
7. What are some significant points of John's letter to Philadelphia?
8. What are some significant points of John's letter to Laodicea?

## For Further Reflection

1. Commentators believe that John is not writing solely to the Churches named in his book, but to the entire Church. Do you find anything in these letters that would apply to the Church today?
2. John repeatedly calls on his listeners to heed what they hear. What message for our own day can we learn from these letters?

# 3
# The Heavenly Vision and the Seven Seals

<table>
<tr>
<td>

Rv 4:
1–6a

‖‖‖‖‖‖‖‖‖‖‖‖‖‖‖‖
</td>
<td>

**4**     *Vision of Heavenly Worship*     ¹After this I had a vision of an open door to heaven, and I heard the trumpet-like voice that had spoken to me before, saying, "Come up here and I will show you what must happen afterwards." ²At once I was caught up in spirit. A throne was there in heaven, and on the throne sat ³one whose appearance sparkled like jasper and carnelian. Around the throne was a halo as brilliant as an emerald. ⁴Surrounding the throne I saw twenty-four other thrones on which twenty-four elders sat, dressed in white garments and with gold crowns on their heads. ⁵From the throne came flashes of lightning, rumblings, and peals of thunder. Seven flaming torches burned in front of the throne, which are the seven spirits of God. ⁶In front of the throne was something that resembled a sea of glass like crystal.
</td>
</tr>
</table>

John now speaks of a new vision. While John previously experienced a vision that seemed to be seen on earth, he is now invited to come into the realm of heaven to see what is hidden beyond the open door. In the Old Testament Book of Ezekiel, we read that the great prophet also saw divine visions through an opening in the heavens (1:1). This was the writer's way of telling his readers that they were about to share in special revelations beyond human experience. A heavenly voice, described as one like a trumpet, invites John to witness what is to take place in the future. Here John writes not of the future of the world, but of the future of the world in which he lives.

In heaven, John sees God, although in accordance with Jewish tradition he does not name God. Instead he identifies him as the One seated on the throne. In the Old Testament, God is described as the One who is enthroned (Ez 1:28; Dn 7:9). The enthroned one is described in images of precious stones (jasper and carnelian), perhaps to avoid likening God to any human being.

In the Book of Ezekiel, we read that the splendor surrounding the Lord was like a rainbow in the sky (1:28). Here, John tells us that a rainbow, like an emerald, surrounded the throne. Around God's throne were twenty-four other thrones on which twenty-four elders sat. The elders, who appear to represent some type of heavenly council, are clothed in white garments and wear gold crowns on their heads, images further alluding to their share in heavenly glory. Just as elders belonged to the powerful councils on earth, so those who belong to the council in heaven are elders. Commentators are unclear as to the significance of the number twenty-four in referring to the number of elders present. Such a number may represent the prophets of the Old Testament, the leaders of the twelve tribes of Israel and the Twelve followers of Jesus, or Christians who have faithfully witnessed to Christ by their lives.

From the throne came forth flashes of lightning and peals of thunder, symbols of God's power at work. Seven torches burned in front of the throne symbolizing the seven lampstands found in the Temple. The seven torches also represent the seven spirits, or guardian angels, of the Churches. These seven spirits show God's dominion over all the earth.

John tells us that the floor surrounding the throne was like a crystal-clear sea of glass. In the story of creation, we read that God separated the upper water above the dome from the water below the dome (Gn 1:6–7). According to the world view of the day, the earth was flat, and God placed a dome on the earth to keep the waters above separate from the waters below. John pictures God as sitting over this water above the dome, and the water appears as if it were a sea of glass beneath his feet. This imagery also signifys God's power over chaos and evil. The Scriptures saw the sea as the abode of chaos and evil, yet, under God's feet, all evil becomes docile and calm.

| Rv 4: 6b–11 | **In the center and around the throne, there were four living creatures covered with eyes in front and in back. [7]The first creature resembled a lion, the second was like a calf, the third had a face like that of a human being, and the fourth looked like an eagle in flight. [8]The four living creatures, each of them with six wings, were covered with eyes inside and out. Day and night they do not stop exclaiming:** |
|---|---|
| | **"Holy, holy, holy is the Lord God almighty, who was, and who is, and who is to come."** |
| | **[9]Whenever the living creatures give glory and honor and** |

thanks to the one who sits on the throne, who lives forever and ever, [10]the twenty-four elders fall down before the one who sits on the throne and worship him, who lives forever and ever. They throw down their crowns before the throne, exclaiming:

[11]"Worthy are you, Lord our God,
    to receive glory and honor and power,
for you created all things;
    because of your will they came to be and were created."

John pictures four living creatures—covered with eyes front and back—surrounding the throne of God. Their multitude of eyes symbolize the creatures' vision and understanding of all. Each of these creatures is symbolized in a different manner: The first creature resembles a lion, the second an ox, the third a human, and the fourth an eagle in flight. Many commentators believe that these symbols were originally images taken from the Babylonian signs of the zodiac. Ezekiel describes four living creatures who had all four faces on each of them (Ez 1:10). Each of the living creatures described in the Book of Revelation also had six wings, similar to the descriptions of the multiwinged creatures found in Ezekiel (1:6) and Isaiah (6:2).

The creatures sing a song of praise to God, proclaiming the holiness of God as the creatures do in Isaiah (6:3). Instead of praising God who "fills heaven and earth" (as found in Isaiah), the creatures use the praise found earlier in the Book of Revelation (1:8), which spoke of a more active image of God, as one "who is, who was and who is to come." At the sound of this praise offered to God, the twenty-four elders, as a sign of their submission, fall prostrate and worship God who lives forever. They throw down their crowns as a sign of total submission to God. They proclaim that the Lord God—as creator of all—is alone worthy of all honor, power, and glory and that all things exist because of God's will.

**Rv 5: 1–8**

**5**    *The Scroll and the Lamb*    [1]I saw a scroll in the right hand of the one who sat on the throne. It had writing on both sides and was sealed with seven seals. [2]Then I saw a mighty angel who proclaimed in a loud voice, "Who is worthy to open the scroll and break its seals?" [3]But no one in heaven or on earth or under the earth was able to open the scroll or to examine it. ⁴I shed many tears because no one was found worthy to open the scroll or to examine it. ⁵One of the elders said to me, "Do not weep. The lion of the tribe of Judah, the root of David, has triumphed, enabling him to open the scroll with its seven seals."

⁶Then I saw standing in the midst of the throne and the four living creatures and the elders, a Lamb that seemed to have been slain. He had seven horns and seven eyes; these are the [seven] spirits of God sent out into the whole world. ⁷He came and received the scroll from the right hand of the one who sat on the throne. ⁸When he took it, the four living creatures and the twenty-four elders fell down before the Lamb. Each of the elders held a harp and gold bowls filled with incense, which are the prayers of the holy ones.

In the right hand of the one who sat on the throne, John saw a scroll that was sealed with seven seals and had writing on both sides of it. The number seven reminds us that the scroll is perfectly sealed. John tells his readers that a mighty angel asks who is worthy of opening the scroll. At the time the letter was written, the people pictured the world as having three tiers: heaven, earth, and the area under the earth. No one in any of these tiers was found worthy of opening the scroll to study its contents.

The image of secret scrolls is found in Old Testament apocalyptic writings. In the Book of Ezekiel, we read that the prophet received a scroll, covered with writing on the front and back, which spoke of lamentation, wailing, and woe (Ez 2:9–10). In the Book of Daniel, we read that the prophet was told to seal the scroll until the end of time (Dn 12:4). John now envisions a scroll to be opened, thus alluding to the arrival of the end times that come with the Second Coming of Christ. The apocalyptic writings of the Old Testament find their fulfillment in the writing of John's apocalypse.

Symbolizing the faithful who wish to have the scroll opened, John weeps because no one is found worthy to open it. An elder tells John not to weep, since the Lion of the tribe of Judah, the Root of David, has conquered and won the right to open the scroll. The Root of David recalls the words of Isaiah 11:1 proclaiming that a shoot shall sprout up from the stump of Jesse, that is, from the offspring of David's father. The offspring points to David and beyond him to Christ, the messianic king. David belongs to the tribe of Judah. The image of Christ as the Lion of the tribe of Judah recalls the prophecy of Jacob as found in the Book of Genesis in which Jacob proclaims that Judah is growing up like a lion's whelp (49:9). Christ is the offspring of the tribe of Judah and the line of David.

John sees a lamb standing between the throne and the four living creatures. Such a position places the lamb closest to the throne over every heavenly creature, thus showing his place of prominence over all. The lamb that John sees is one that has been slain, a reference to the death and resurrection of Jesus. It also recalls the words of Isaiah who spoke of the one who was to come as being like a lamb led to the slaughter (Is 53:7). The lamb seen by John has seven horns (an image with signified power) and seven eyes. John tells us the eyes—which see all and know all—are the seven spirits sent to all parts of the world. The number seven signifies the perfection of the lamb's power (horns) and knowledge (eyes).

When the lamb takes the scroll from the one seated on the throne, the four living creatures and the twenty-four elders fall down in worship, recognizing that the lamb shares in the power and glory of God. In the previous chapter, the twenty-four elders had fallen prostrate as the heavenly creatures praised God (4:8–10), and they now do the same before the lamb. Harps were used to sing the psalms and give praise to God. In this imagery presented by John, those who prostrate themselves before the lamb carry harps as symbols of their praise and have bowls of gold brimming with perfumed spices. These bowls symbolize the prayers and supplications of the all-faithful Christians (the saints) as they raise their prayer to God.

|           |
|-----------|
| **Rv 5:** |
| **9–14**  |

⁹They sang a new hymn:

"**Worthy are you to receive the scroll**
   **and to break open its seals,**
      **for you were slain and with your blood you purchased for God**
      **those from every tribe and tongue, people and nation.**
¹⁰**You made them a kingdom and priests for our God,**
   **and they will reign on earth.**"
¹¹I looked again and heard the voices of many angels who surrounded the throne and the living creatures and the elders. They were countless in number, ¹²and they cried out in a loud voice:

"**Worthy is the Lamb that was slain**
   **to receive power and riches, wisdom and strength,**
   **honor and glory and blessing.**"
¹³Then I heard every creature in heaven and on earth

and under the earth and in the sea, everything in the universe, cry out:

"To the one who sits on the throne and to the Lamb
be blessing and honor, glory and might,
forever and ever."

[14]The four living creatures answered, "Amen," and the elders fell down and worshiped.

In the Book of Isaiah, the prophet speaks of singing a new song to the Lord, as the Lord's glory and power are made manifest (42:10). In the same way, John tells us that the heavenly court sings a new song in honor of the lamb, proclaiming that he is worthy to break the seals because he purchased people from every race and nation for God. These images of race, tongue, people, and nation were used in John's time to designate all the peoples of the world. Those who follow the lamb entered into a kingdom and were made priests to serve God. Since God has everything on earth under control, those who are faithful shall reign in God's kingdom on earth.

As the vision continues, all those in the heavenly court—the angels, the living creatures, the elders, tens of thousands—all join in to praise the lamb. When the author uses the number "a thousand" or any variation of it, he is telling us that a countless amount is involved in the activity described. In this case, they are involved in worshiping the lamb and in proclaiming the lamb's power, wealth, wisdom and strength and his honor, glory and blessing.

The setting in this passage now moves from the heavenly court praising the lamb to the creatures of the whole universe—in heaven, on earth, under the earth, and in the seas—joining in praise of the One who sits on the throne as well as in praise of the lamb. The creatures add their "Amen" to this dramatic and universal clamor of praise, and the elders again fall down in worship.

Rv 6:
1–8

**6    The First Six Seals**    [1]Then I watched while the Lamb broke open the first of the seven seals, and I heard one of the four living creatures cry out in a voice like thunder, "Come forward." [2]I looked, and there was a white horse, and its rider had a bow. He was given a crown, and he rode forth victorious to further his victories.

[3]When he broke open the second seal, I heard the second living creature cry out, "Come forward." [4]Another

horse came out, a red one. Its rider was given power to take peace away from the earth, so that people would slaughter one another. And he was given a huge sword.

5When he broke open the third seal, I heard the third living creature cry out, "Come forward." I looked, and there was a black horse, and its rider held a scale in his hand. 6I heard what seemed to be a voice in the midst of the four living creatures. It said, "A ration of wheat costs a day's pay, and three rations of barley cost a day's pay. But do not damage the olive oil or the wine."

7When he broke open the fourth seal, I heard the voice of the fourth living creature cry out, "Come forward." 8I looked, and there was a pale green horse. Its rider was named Death, and Hades accompanied him. They were given authority over a quarter of the earth, to kill with sword, famine, and plague, and by means of the beasts of the earth.

When the seals are broken, the scrolls are not read, but they become an instrument of living instruction. Out of the scrolls come the famous four horsemen, each with his own message, yet dependent on one another. In reading about each of the four horsemen, readers should avoid misinterpreting these events as taking place one after the other; rather, they should be viewed as occurring siumultaneously. Much of the Book of Revelation should be read in this same fashion: an image of the end time is presented and events are described in sequence, yet the same message is being relayed from different viewpoints.

Most commentators believe that the image of the four horsemen found here is strongly influenced by the Book of Zechariah (1:8–15; 6:1–8). In these passages, Zechariah speaks of the Lord sending out horsemen, who drive chariots pulled by different colored horses. The horses and their drivers were sent out to patrol the earth for the Lord. In the Book of Revelation, the horsemen and their horses signal some type of destruction for the world.

When the lamb breaks open the first seal, one of the four creatures around the throne calls out the command, "Come forward!" To the surprise of the author, a white horse comes out with a rider carrying a bow, and the rider receives a crown. The white horse and the crown were signs of victory, while many commentators view the bow as a symbol of the army of Parthians, a strong nation from the east and a threat to the power of the Roman Empire. The Parthians were particularly famous for their use of the bow as a weapon in war. John, in an attempt to read the sign of the times, mistakenly envisions the Parthians as conquering the Roman Empire.

When the lamb breaks open the second seal, the second living creature calls forth a red horse whose rider is given the power to destroy peace on the earth by slaughtering the people of many nations. For this slaughter, the rider is given a great sword. The red horse signifies bloodshed, and the image signifies the ravages of war that will encompass the earth.

When the lamb opens the third seal, the third living creature calls forth a black horse with a rider who holds a pair of scales in his hands. John hears a voice that sounds as if it is coming from the midst of the four creatures. The voice cries out that a ration of wheat or three rations of barley cost a denarius, that is, a day's wages. This amount of wheat would only be sufficient to feed one person. The reason for the high cost of wheat is shown in the second part of the message when the voice cries out that the wine and the oil should be spared. The reason for the high cost of wheat and barley, therefore, lay in their scarcity. The Roman Empire, intent on having wine and oil, paid high prices for these commodities; but a landowner would yield a greater profit from growing grapes and olives than he would from wheat and barley. Such were the agricultural circumstances leading to famine in the land.

When the lamb breaks open the fourth seal, the fourth living creature exposed was a sickly, pale green horse. The rider of the horse is death, and the world of the dead rides with him. These four horses and horsemen together were given the authority to overrun one fourth of the earth, killing people with war, famine, sickness, and wild beasts. As mentioned earlier, these events would occur simultaneously, not one right after another.

**Rv 6: 9–17**

⁹**When he broke open the fifth seal, I saw underneath the altar the souls of those who had been slaughtered because of the witness they bore to the word of God. ¹⁰They cried out in a loud voice, "How long will it be, holy and true master, before you sit in judgment and avenge our blood on the inhabitants of the earth?" ¹¹Each of them was given a white robe, and they were told to be patient a little while longer until the number was filled of their fellow servants and brothers who were going to be killed as they had been.**

¹²**Then I watched while he broke open the sixth seal, and there was a great earthquake; the sun turned as black as dark sackcloth and the whole moon became like blood.**

<sup>13</sup>The stars in the sky fell to the earth like unripe figs
shaken loose from the tree in a strong wind. <sup>14</sup>Then the
sky was divided like a torn scroll curling up, and every
mountain and island was moved from its place. <sup>15</sup>The kings
of the earth, the nobles, the military officers, the rich, the
powerful, and every slave and free person hid themselves
in caves and among mountain crags. <sup>16</sup>They cried out to
the mountains and the rocks, "Fall on us and hide us from
the face of the one who sits on the throne and from the
wrath of the Lamb, <sup>17</sup>because the great day of their wrath
has come and who can withstand it?"

When the lamb breaks open the fifth seal, John sees under the altar the
spirits of those who have been martyred. Their martyrdom was the result of
their witnessing to God, and they now cry out, asking how long they must
wait for God's vengeance on the injustices of the world. We as readers
should not misconstrue this outcry as one given in a spirit of revenge, but
rather one of calling for justice.

The people of John's day wonder how long God will allow the power
of evil to remain in control. The fact that the martyrs are pictured as being
under the altar signifies their part as the perfect sacrifice offered to God.
All of the martyrs are given white robes as an assurance that they can claim
a share in heavenly glory, but they are also urged to be patient until their
number has reached its completion. This idea follows the Jewish mentality
that God has already established the number of those who will share in the
abode of the dead. The author carries the idea a step further, speaking of
those who will be sharing in eternal glory. The stating of a number does not
mean to set a limit, but instead establishes a number as the number for
completion or fulfillment.

When the lamb opens the sixth seal, catastrophes in the skies and on
the earth begin to occur. Such catastrophes are a part of all apocalyptic
writing, and many of the events described here are found in apocalyptic
writings of the Old Testament. Pointing to a day of judgment, these
catastrophes include earthquakes, darkness, changes in the moon's color,
stars falling from the sky, the sky collapsing, and mountains and islands
tearing away from their foundations. The day of judgment will be a
frightening day of vengeance for those who have not properly used the gifts
of this world. They recognize that the punishment in store for them is so
great that they would rather face sudden death and oblivion than the wrath
of God. They call out to the mountains to crush them and hide them from
God. Judgment Day, however, will come, and no one can escape it.

**Rv 7: 1–8**

**7**   *The 144,000 Sealed*   [1]After this I saw four angels standing at the four corners of the earth, holding back the four winds of the earth so that no wind could blow on land or sea or against any tree. [2]Then I saw another angel come up from the East, holding the seal of the living God. He cried out in a loud voice to the four angels who were given power to damage the land and the sea, [3]"Do not damage the land or the sea or the trees until we put the seal on the foreheads of the servants of our God." [4]I heard the number of those who had been marked with the seal, one hundred and forty-four thousand marked from every tribe of the Israelites: [5]twelve thousand were marked from the tribe of Judah, twelve thousand from the tribe of Reuben, twelve thousand from the tribe of Gad, [6]twelve thousand from the tribe of Asher, twelve thousand from the tribe of Naphtali, twelve thousand from the tribe of Manasseh, [7]twelve thousand from the tribe of Simeon, twelve thousand from the tribe of Levi, twelve thousand from the tribe of Issachar, [8]twelve thousand from the tribe of Zebulun, twelve thousand from the tribe of Joseph, and twelve thousand were marked from the tribe of Benjamin.

John pictures the world as a flat earth with four sides. At each corner, he sees four angels holding back the four winds which have the power to damage the land, sea, and earth. Coming up from the east, the place of sunrise, another angel calls out to the four angels to hold back the winds from damaging the earth until he has had a chance to mark the servants of God. These are the ones who will be spared.

The idea of marking the servants of the Lord has appeared before in the Scriptures. On the night of the first Passover, when the people of Israel were preparing to escape from Egypt under the leadership of Moses, they were instructed to paint the blood of a lamb on their doorposts so that the angel of death would pass them by and kill only the firstborn of the families in the unmarked homes (Ex 12:21–23). In the Book of Ezekiel, we read of six men who came to destroy the people of Jerusalem. Ahead of them went a man in white linen who marked an X on the foreheads of those who mourned the abominations practiced within the city. The six men were to kill all the people except those who were marked with the X (Ez 9:1–7). In the same way, the angel from the east used a huge seal of the living God to mark those who were to be saved.

John states that he heard the number to be saved was one hundred and forty-four thousand. In ancient writings, numbers given in thousands usually pointed to a multitude of people too large to be counted. The one hundred and forty-four comes from twelve multiplied by twelve. Many attempts to explain the significance of this number have been offered. Some commentators believe that it represented the number of the twelve tribes of the Old Testament Israel multiplied by the number of the twelve Apostles chosen by Christ, who are represented as the leaders of the New Israel. The message would then state that a countless amount of people from the old and new covenants would be saved. Other commentators believe that the number simply represents those who are faithful followers of Christ, the true Israelites who belong to the Chosen People because of their faith. Some people have even taken the number literally, falsely interpreting it to mean that only one hundred and forty-four thousand people would be saved.

John names twelve tribes of Israel with twelve thousand saved from each of the tribes. With the exception of Manasseh, a son of Joseph and a grandson of Jacob, all the tribes receive their names from the sons of Jacob. The list begins with the tribe of Judah. Although Judah is not the oldest of the sons, he is named first because the messiah is to come from the tribe of Judah. Those familiar with the names of the twelve sons of Jacob will notice that the tribe bearing the name of Jacob's son, Dan, is missing. The reason for this omission appears to stem from a belief that the Antichrist will come from this tribe. With the tribe of Dan missing, John chooses a grandson of Jacob—Manasseh—as the name of a tribe to replace that of Dan.

| Rv 7: 9–8:1 | *Triumph of the Elect*     **⁹After this I had a vision of a great multitude, which no one could count, from every nation, race, people, and tongue. They stood before the throne and before the Lamb, wearing white robes and holding palm branches in their hands. ¹⁰They cried out in a loud voice:** |

**"Salvation comes from our God, who is seated on the throne,**

**and from the Lamb."**

**¹¹All the angels stood around the throne and around the elders and the four living creatures. They prostrated themselves before the throne, worshiped God, ¹²and exclaimed:**

"Amen. Blessing and glory, wisdom and thanksgiving,
    honor, power, and might
        be to our God forever and ever. Amen."

[13]Then one of the elders spoke up and said to me,
"Who are these wearing white robes, and where did they
come from?" [14]I said to him, "My lord, you are the one
who knows." He said to me, "These are the ones who have
survived the time of great distress; they have washed their
robes and made them white in the blood of the Lamb.

[15]"For this reason they stand before God's throne
    and worship him day and night in his temple.
The one who sits on the throne will shelter them.
[16]They will not hunger or thirst anymore,
    nor will the sun or any heat strike them.
[17]For the Lamb who is in the center of the throne will
        shepherd them
    and lead them to springs of life-giving water,
    and God will wipe away every tear from their eyes."

**8**    *The Seven Trumpets*    [1]When he broke open the
seventh seal, there was silence in heaven for about half an
hour.

John now turns his attention to the elect who stand before the throne and
the lamb. John sees a huge throng of people, too numerous to count, who
have come from every group in creation (every nation, race, people, and
tongue). They stand before the throne, dressed in white robes and holding
palm branches, two signs of their victorious state. Since they cannot
personally claim any power for this victory, they cry out that all salvation
comes from God, the One seated on the throne, and from the lamb, who is
Jesus Christ. The whole heavenly court answers this prayer by falling
prostrate and proclaiming as a response their "Amen." They answer a
second "Amen" to their own prayer of praise, thanksgiving, and glory to
God.

In explaining the vision, John uses a technique common in apocalyptic
writings. He has one of the elders ask him who these people are, and when
he is unable to answer, the elder gives the interpretation, explaining to
John that the people are those who have survived the great time of trial.
Like Christ, the lamb who came to victory through death, these people are

the martyrs who have been washed clean in the blood of the Lamb. They have suffered in union with Christ.

John uses liturgical symbols to describe the activity of these elect around the throne. They serve in the Temple day and night, while the one who sits on the throne protects them. Old Testament images are used to show the security and happiness found in heaven. The Book of Isaiah speaks of freeing the Israelites from hunger, thirst, and the scorching wind and sun (49:10). John applies this text to the elect who find themselves free from these trials. Recalling many Old Testament texts that speak of the Lord as a shepherd, John states that the lamb on the throne shall shepherd them (see Is 40:11; Ezek 34:23). He shall lead them to springs of living waters (see Jer 2:13), and God will wipe every tear from their eyes (see Is 25:8).

In the seventh chapter, John makes use of a short interlude before telling us what happened when the lamb opened the seventh seal. The eighth chapter begins with the opening of the seventh seal, and a dramatic silence, lasting a half hour, follows the opening of this final seal. Commentators disagree on the specific meaning of this silence, but some suspect the silence is simply a dramatic way to build up the reader's anticipation of events to come. The opening of the seventh seal begins a new series of visions, the visions of the seven trumpets.

# Review

1. What is the significance of the heavenly vision that John sees through the open door to heaven?
2. Who are the four living creatures and the elders?
3. What is the significance of the lamb and the seven seals?
4. What is the meaning of the four different colored horses that emerge when the first four seals are broken?
5. What catastrophes occur after the sixth seal is opened?
6. How does John picture the elect in the heavenly court?
7. What happens when the seventh seal is broken?

# For Further Reflection

1. The lamb who was slain was alone worthy to open the seals. What message do we receive for our lives today from this story of the lamb who was slain?

2. The messages found in the opening of each of the seven seals is meant to offer hope to the readers of these words. How do we find hope today in the message behind the opening of the seven seals?

3. John tells us that one hundred and forty-four thousand will be among the elect. What message of hope do these words offer us today?

# 4
# The Seven Trumpets

Rv 8:
2–5

²And I saw that the seven angels who stood before God were given seven trumpets.

*The Gold Censer* ³Another angel came and stood at the altar, holding a gold censer. He was given a great quantity of incense to offer, along with the prayers of all the holy ones, on the gold altar that was before the throne. ⁴The smoke of the incense along with the prayers of the holy ones went up before God from the hand of the angel. ⁵Then the angel took the censer, filled it with burning coals from the altar, and hurled it down to the earth. There were peals of thunder, rumblings, flashes of lightning, and an earthquake.

Seven trumpets, which mark the beginning of a new series of visions, are given to the seven angels who are ministering in God's presence. Another angel takes his place at the altar of incense, holding a censer of gold in his hand. The angel adds a large amount of incense to the prayers of the martyrs who (as we have been told earlier) are under the altar. The incense is a symbol of the purity of the prayers being offered before God. The angel fills the censer with fire from the altar (a symbol of the fire of God's judgment) and casts it down to earth. Thunder and lightning shake the earth. Such images are often used as expressions of God's wrath.

Rv 8:
6–13

*The First Four Trumpets* ⁶The seven angels who were holding the seven trumpets prepared to blow them.

⁷When the first one blew his trumpet, there came hail and fire mixed with blood, which was hurled down to the earth. A third of the land was burned up, along with a third of the trees and all green grass.

⁸When the second angel blew his trumpet, something like a large burning mountain was hurled into the sea. A

third of the sea turned to blood, [9]a third of the creatures living in the sea died, and a third of the ships were wrecked.

[10]When the third angel blew his trumpet, a large star burning like a torch fell from the sky. It fell on a third of the rivers and on the springs of water. [11]The star was called "Wormwood," and a third of all the water turned to wormwood. Many people died from this water, because it was made bitter.

[12]When the fourth angel blew his trumpet, a third of the sun, a third of the moon, and a third of the stars were struck, so that a third of them became dark. The day lost its light for a third of the time, as did the night.

[13]Then I looked again and heard an eagle flying high overhead cry out in a loud voice, "Woe! Woe! Woe to the inhabitants of the earth from the rest of the trumpet blasts that the three angels are about to blow!"

John pictures the seven angels with the seven trumpets, poised and ready to blow them. Each time an angel blows the trumpet, a catastrophe occurs causing damage to the world or its inhabitants. This series of catastrophes is not related to the visions following the breaking of the seals. The visions following the trumpet blasts are other views of God's judgment of the world.

John has the first four trumpet blasts herald some destruction for the world, while the last three blasts will directly affect human beings. In the events described with the first four trumpet blasts, readers will recognize many plagues that resemble those found in Egypt during Moses' time.

The first angel blows his trumpet, and hail, fire, and blood fall on the earth. While Moses was in Egypt, hail rained down on the people of Egypt, causing destruction for the people and their crops (Ex 9:23–26). This first trumpet blast brings destruction to earth, scorching a third of the land with a third of the trees and green plants.

The second trumpet blast causes something resembling a huge mountain to be cast into the sea in flames. Here, John may be refering to an erupting volcano as it rises to great heights and sends lava down into the waters. This trumpet blast turns a third of the sea to blood, as the Nile was turned to blood during Moses' time (Ex 7:20). A third of the ships were wrecked, and a third of the fish died from the resulting pollution. This second trumpet blast caused destruction on the sea.

The third trumpet blast sends a flaming star crashing into the fresh waters of the earth, causing them to become bitter. The name of this star, "Wormwood," recalls passages from Jeremiah that speak of the Lord giving wormwood to the people to eat and poison to drink (Jer 23:15). This star pollutes the water, and a third of it turns to poison, killing many people. This trumpet blast affects the fresh streams and rivers.

The fourth trumpet blast affects the firmament. A third of the sun, a third of the moon, and a third of the stars are struck hard enough to cause the day and night to lose a third of its light. During the time of Moses in Egypt, one of the plagues consisted of darkness covering the earth (Ex 10:21). The loss of light in the firmament recalls this plague.

After presenting the trumpet blasts given by the first four angels, John makes use of a dramatic interlude before proceeding with the remainder of the trumpets. He pictures an eagle soaring overhead and crying out three woes that will follow for the people of the earth when the next three trumpet blasts sound.

| Rv 9: 1–12 | **9**    *The Fifth Trumpet*    ¹**Then the fifth angel blew his trumpet, and I saw a star that had fallen from the sky to the earth. It was given the key for the passage to the abyss. ²It opened the passage to the abyss, and smoke came up out of the passage like smoke from a huge furnace. The sun and the air were darkened by the smoke from the passage. ³Locusts came out of the smoke onto the land, and they were given the same power as scorpions of the earth. ⁴They were told not to harm the grass of the earth or any plant or any tree, but only those people who did not have the seal of God on their foreheads. ⁵They were not allowed to kill them but only to torment them for five months; the torment they inflicted was like that of a scorpion when it stings a person. ⁶During that time these people will seek death but will not find it, and they will long to die but death will escape them.** |
|---|---|

**⁷The appearance of the locusts was like that of horses ready for battle. On their heads they wore what looked like crowns of gold; their faces were like human faces, ⁸and they had hair like women's hair. Their teeth were like lions' teeth, ⁹and they had chests like iron breastplates. The sound of their wings was like the sound of many**

horse-drawn chariots racing into battle. **¹⁰They had tails like scorpions, with stingers; with their tails they had power to harm people for five months. ¹¹They had as their king the angel of the abyss, whose name in Hebrew is Abaddon and in Greek Apollyon.**

**¹²The first woe has passed, but there are two more to come.**

When the fifth angel blows the trumpet, a star falls from heaven. Early Jewish literature portrayed the stars as angels, and the image presented here is that God sends an angel with a key to open a bottomless pit. Although the author speaks of a star that falls from heaven, he may be referring simply to an angel who descends from heaven to perform a task for God. Some commentators see in the star an image of the fallen angel. The bottomless pit is not the abode of the dead, but the abode of those evil spirits who are suffering punishment.

When the angel opens the bottomless pit, dark smoke, like that from a furnace, billows out of the pit and it covers the sun and fills the air with its darkness. Out of this smoke emerges a type of locust unknown on this earth. These locusts had tails which stung like scorpions, and they were ordered not to destroy the grass, plants, or trees (as locusts ordinarily do). The horde of locusts recalls the eighth plague in the Book of Exodus that speaks of locusts overrunning the land (10:4–15). The image of locusts used here closely parallels the Book of Joel which speaks in its opening chapters of the "Day of the Lord," marked by the coming of many locusts.

The sting of the scorpion was a frightening and well-known affliction for the people who lived near warm, desert regions. Although a sting produced by the tail of the locusts would not bring death as with a scorpion sting, the pain would be so great that death would actually be desired. Primarily using the description from the Book of Joel, John pictures the locusts lined in battle array, wearing the crown of victory. They have human faces, long hair in the image of barbarian invaders, the teeth of lions, and chests like iron breastplates. Their wings sound like charging chariots and horses in battle, and their scorpionlike tails have the power to cause pain for a period of five months. Five months is the usual seasonal span for the locust. Like any army, the locusts have a leader, a king, who is the ruler of the abyss. His Hebrew name is Abaddon and his Greek name is Appollyon. Both of these words translate as "destruction," and the author personifies Destruction to add credibility to the scenario, which concludes the first of the three woes.

<table>
<tr><td>

**Rv 9:
13–21**

‖‖‖‖‖‖‖‖‖‖‖‖‖‖‖‖‖

</td><td>

*The Sixth Trumpet*      **¹³Then the sixth angel blew his
trumpet, and I heard a voice coming from the [four] horns
of the gold altar before God, ¹⁴telling the sixth angel who
held the trumpet, "Release the four angels who are bound
at the banks of the great river Euphrates." ¹⁵So the four
angels were released, who were prepared for this hour,
day, month, and year to kill a third of the human race.
¹⁶The number of cavalry troops was two hundred million; I
heard their number. ¹⁷Now in my vision this is how I saw
the horses and their riders. They wore red, blue, and yel-
low breastplates, and the horses' heads were like heads of
lions, and out of their mouths came fire, smoke, and sul-
fur. ¹⁸By these three plagues of fire, smoke, and sulfur that
came out of their mouths a third of the human race was
killed. ¹⁹For the power of the horses is in their mouths and
in their tails; for their tails are like snakes, with heads that
inflict harm.**

**²⁰The rest of the human race, who were not killed by
these plagues, did not repent of the works of their hands,
to give up the worship of demons and idols made from
gold, silver, bronze, stone, and wood, which cannot see or
hear or walk. ²¹Nor did they repent of their murders, their
magic potions, their unchastity, or their robberies.**

</td></tr>
</table>

With a warning that only the first woe has passed and that two more are to
follow, the author moves on to the second woe. When the sixth angel
blows the trumpet, a voice calls out from the four horns (corners) of the
altar in God's presence. This imagery reminds us of the martyrs under the
altar who called for God's justice on the evildoers of the world (6:9–11).
The voice that spoke in God's presence ordered the sixth angel to untie the
four angels bound at the great river Euphrates. Their bondage shows that a
greater power was able to both bind them and loose them at will. The
Euphrates river was located at the eastern end of the empire and separated
it from the powerful Parthians. Although John may possibly be referring to
the expected invasion of the Parthians, he speaks of a mythological
invasion, like that of the locusts, in which the horses, and not the humans,
are the destructive force. Kept in check by God until the specific hour, day,
month, and year, the horses would then thunder out to kill a third of all
humankind.

The number of the invaders is astronomical. John tells us that he heard the number was two hundred million. He describes the breastplates of the riders in apocalyptic colors of fiery red, deep blue and yellow. John now turns his attention to the horses that will cause the real destruction. With heads like lions, they spewed out of their mouths fire, sulphur, and smoke, which slew a third of all the people. Like the locusts, they had serpents for tails, ready to strike.

Although these afflictions were meant to lead to repentance, those who escaped the invasion did not repent but continued to worship demons or idols made of mere material ornaments, such as gold, silver, bronze, stone, and wood. Since these gods did not really exist, John tells us that they are gods who cannot see, hear, or walk. Murder, witchcraft, fornication, and stealing continued as a natural result of idolatry.

**Rv 10: 1–11**

**10**    *The Angel with the Small Scroll*    [1]**Then I saw another mighty angel come down from heaven wrapped in a cloud, with a halo around his head; his face was like the sun and his feet were like pillars of fire.** [2]**In his hand he held a small scroll that had been opened. He placed his right foot on the sea and his left foot on the land,** [3]**and then he cried out in a loud voice as a lion roars. When he cried out, the seven thunders raised their voices, too.** [4]**When the seven thunders had spoken, I was about to write it down; but I heard a voice from heaven say, "Seal up what the seven thunders have spoken, but do not write it down."** [5]**Then the angel I saw standing on the sea and on the land raised his right hand to heaven** [6]**and swore by the one who lives forever and ever, who created heaven and earth and sea and all that is in them, "There shall be no more delay.** [7]**At the time when you hear the seventh angel blow his trumpet, the mysterious plan of God shall be fulfilled, as he promised to his servants the prophets."**

[8]**Then the voice that I had heard from heaven spoke to me again and said, "Go, take the scroll that lies open in the hand of the angel who is standing on the sea and on the land."** [9]**So I went up to the angel and told him to give me the small scroll. He said to me, "Take and swallow it. It will turn your stomach sour, but in your mouth it will taste as sweet as honey."** [10]**I took the small scroll from**

the angel's hand and swallowed it. In my mouth it was like sweet honey, but when I had eaten it, my stomach turned sour. [11]Then someone said to me, "You must prophesy again about many peoples, nations, tongues, and kings."

Just as John added a small interlude between the opening of the sixth and seventh seals, he now adds another between the sixth and seventh trumpets. He describes a vision of a great angel, possibly a reference to the Angel Gabriel, who comes to him from heaven. In this chapter, John reworks images found in the opening chapters of the Book of Ezekiel. The angel is wrapped in a cloud (Ez 1:4), with a rainbow about his head (Ez 1:28); he has a shining face like one who lives in God's presence, and legs like pillars of fire. These are all scriptural signs of a heavenly visitation.

The angel holds a smaller scroll in his hand, and he stands with one foot on the sea and one on the land, a symbol that he is covering the whole earth (both land and sea). At the roar of the angel, which sounds like a lion's roar, seven thunders add their voices to that of the angel. In scriptural imagery, God speaks to the people by means of thunder. The number seven used here may refer to the seven spirits speaking, or possibly to the completeness of the message. Just as John prepares to write down what he hears, he is told to seal up what he has heard from the seven thunders and not to record it. These instructions to John may possibly serve to point out to the reader that, although John has received the total revelation from God, the reader is not privileged to receive the full revelation; indeed, the revelation shared here is incomplete.

Standing above the whole earth, the great angel swears by God, the Creator of all, that the seventh angel should now blow the trumpet. When the angel does so, God's plan, given to the prophets, will be fully accomplished. The angel's words here add to the suspense surrounding the seventh trumpet.

The voice that John first heard from heaven tells him to take the scroll from the angel standing over all the earth. When he does so, the angel tells him to take the scroll and eat it. These words recall the message given to Ezekiel when God told him to take the scroll and eat it (Ez 2:8–3:4). The scroll tastes sweet to John, just as it had to Ezekiel. After John eats the scroll, however, it becomes bitter to his stomach. John provides this description to inform his readers that they will receive the message of Jesus Christ as something sweet to the taste but that they will live in pain as they digest it and live by its message. Just as Ezekiel is told to preach the Word of God after he eats the scroll (Ez 3:4), so John is given the commission to go out and preach to all the world (peoples, nations, tongues, and kings).

**Rv 11: 1–14**

**11    *The Two Witnesses*** [1]Then I was given a measuring rod like a staff and I was told, "Come and measure the temple of God and the altar, and count those who are worshiping in it. [2]But exclude the outer court of the temple; do not measure it, for it has been handed over to the Gentiles, who will trample the holy city for forty-two months. [3]I will commission my two witnesses to prophesy for those twelve hundred and sixty days, wearing sackcloth." [4]These are the two olive trees and the two lampstands that stand before the Lord of the earth. [5]If anyone wants to harm them, fire comes out of their mouths and devours their enemies. In this way, anyone wanting to harm them is sure to be slain. [6]They have the power to close up the sky so that no rain can fall during the time of their prophesying. They also have power to turn water into blood and to afflict the earth with any plague as often as they wish.

[7]When they have finished their testimony, the beast that comes up from the abyss will wage war against them and conquer them and kill them. [8]Their corpses will lie in the main street of the great city, which has the symbolic names "Sodom" and "Egypt," where indeed their Lord was crucified. [9]Those from every people, tribe, tongue, and nation will gaze on their corpses for three and a half days, and they will not allow their corpses to be buried. [10]The inhabitants of the earth will gloat over them and be glad and exchange gifts because these two prophets tormented the inhabitants of the earth. [11]But after the three and a half days, a breath of life from God entered them. When they stood on their feet, great fear fell on those who saw them. [12]Then they heard a loud voice from heaven say to them, "Come up here." So they went up to heaven in a cloud as their enemies looked on. [13]At that moment there was a great earthquake, and a tenth of the city fell in ruins. Seven thousand people were killed during the earth-

quake; the rest were terrified and gave glory to the God of heaven.

<sup>14</sup>The second woe has passed, but the third is coming soon.

Drawing heavily on previous apocalyptic writings, this interlude is one of the most difficult sections to interpret in the Book of Revelation. In the Book of Ezekiel, the prophet is told to measure the Temple and the altar (40–43). At the beginning of this chapter of Revelations, John tells us that someone has given him a measuring rod, instructing him to measure God's Temple and the altar and to count the number of those who worship there. He is told not to measure the outer court, the place where the non-Jews were allowed to gather. The voice tells John that this area will be turned over to the invading armies. The measured area, which will apparently be protected, may refer to the remnant of those "true Jews" (Gentiles as well as Jews) who have accepted Christ's message. The invaders will ravage the holy city for forty-two months. The number of months adds up to three and a half years, which is half of seven, the perfect number. This serves as a symbol of an incomplete and transitory period of time indicating the power of evil is to be incomplete and limited. John tells us that two witnesses, wearing sackcloth, the clothing of repentance, will witness to God during the period of twelve hundred and sixty days.

John chooses images from the Book of Zechariah and from other prophets to describe the mission of the two witnesses. In a vision in the Book of Zechariah, the prophet speaks of seven lamps and two olive trees located to the right and the left of the lamps. An angel tells Zechariah that these olive trees are the two anointed who stand beside the Lord of the entire earth (Zec 4:12–14). Similarly, John pictures two olive trees and two lampstands that stand in the presence of the Lord. These are the two witnesses who continue to be described in apocalyptic terms. John borrows another image from the Second Book of Kings that recalls Elijah as he calls down fire on the messengers of the king of Samaria (2 Kg 1:10–15). In the same way here, the heavenly messenger tells John that anyone who attempts to harm these witnesses will face a similar destruction.

John once again alludes to an event in Elijah's life when he tells us that the witnesses have the power to close up the sky so that it will not rain during the time of their mission. In the First Book of Kings, God gives Elijah the power to determine when rain or dew will come upon the earth (1 Kg 17:1). Another power given to these witnesses recalls an event from the Book of Exodus where the Nile is turned to blood (Ex 7:14–19). Similarly, the witnesses here will have the power to turn water into blood and to inflict other plagues on the earth.

Based on John's choice of references, many commentators identify these witnesses as Elijah and Moses. Many of the Jewish people expected Elijah to return before the coming of the Messiah, and some expected Moses to return in a new, prophetic role. In the Book of Revelation, they would be the heralds of the Second Coming of Christ.

After these witnesses perform their special mission, the wild beast from the abyss wages war against them and kills them. Their bodies lie in the street for three and a half days, the allotted time for evil to work. In ancient times, it was considered a shameful end not to have one's body buried, since it not only contaminated the name of the unburied people but also the city in which their corpses lay. Their bodies lay in the streets of the great city, which the author calls "Sodom" and "Egypt," and which most commentators see as a reference to Jerusalem, where (as the author states) Jesus was crucified. A time of rejoicing and gift sharing expresses the relief of the people of the world who disapproved of the message preached against them by the witnesses. After the three and a half days allotted to the power of evil had transpired, the Lord breathes life into the witnesses, sending fear into the hearts of those who saw them. A voice from heaven calls the witnesses, and they ascend to heaven in a cloud within sight of their enemies. In the Second Book of Kings, we read that Elijah ascended to heaven (2 Kg 2:11), and early Jewish legends spoke of Moses being taken up. John is likely drawing on both of these beliefs when he speaks of the witnesses being taken into heaven.

The earth immediately receives God's wrath in the form of a shattering earthquake that destroys a tenth of the city and kills seven thousand people. In terror, the survivors turn to worship God in heaven. John states that the second woe has now passed, but he warns that the third is soon to come.

---

**Rv 11: 15–19**

***The Seventh Trumpet*** [15]Then the seventh angel blew his trumpet. There were loud voices in heaven, saying, "The kingdom of the world now belongs to our Lord and to his Anointed, and he will reign forever and ever." [16]The twenty-four elders who sat on their thrones before God prostrated themselves and worshiped God [17]and said:

"We give thanks to you, Lord God almighty,
  who are and who were.
For you have assumed your great power
  and have established your reign.

$^{18}$The nations raged,
>     but your wrath has come,
>     and the time for the dead to be judged,
> and to recompense your servants, the prophets,
>     and the holy ones and those who fear your name,
>     the small and the great alike,
> and to destroy those who destroy the earth."

$^{19}$Then God's temple in heaven was opened, and the ark of his covenant could be seen in the temple. There were flashes of lightning, rumblings, and peals of thunder, an earthquake, and a violent hailstorm.

When the seventh angel blows his horn, loud voices in heaven proclaim that the kingdom now belongs to the Lord and to Christ, the Anointed One, who shall rule for all eternity. The kingdom of Satan has come to an end. The twenty-four elders fall prostrate and praise God, who is and who was. Since they are celebrating the end of the world, the elders do not include "who is to come," as they had done in the past. They proclaim that the reign of God has begun. Nations tried to rebel against the Lord, but the day of God's wrath has come. It is time to judge the dead, to reward the faithful prophets and the saints, and to destroy those who destroyed the earth.

When God opens the Temple, John sees the Ark of the Covenant. The Ark was lost when the first Temple was destroyed, and Jewish legend taught that it would return in the messianic age. Lightning, thunder, earthquakes, and hailstorms accompany this vision, signaling the reader that John is experiencing his vision in God's presence.

# Review

1. What is the symbol behind the altar of incense and the live coals cast down on the earth?
2. What happened when the first four trumpets were blown?
3. What is the meaning of the vision of the locusts who come on the scene when the fifth trumpet is blown?
4. What is the meaning of the vision that follows the blowing of the sixth trumpet?
5. What message do we receive from the story of the angel with the open scroll?
6. What is the message behind measuring the Temple and the two witnesses?
7. What happens when the seventh trumpet is blown?

# For Further Reflection

1. The seven trumpets come forth from the seventh seal. What message can we receive for our lives from the story of the seven trumpets?
2. The scroll that tastes like honey and becomes bitter in the stomach refers to the Christian message which is easy to receive, but hard to live out. How can we apply this message to our lives today?

# 5
# The Unnumbered Visions

Rv 12: 1–6

**12**  *The Woman and the Dragon*  [1]A great sign appeared in the sky, a woman clothed with the sun, with the moon under her feet, and on her head a crown of twelve stars. [2]She was with child and wailed aloud in pain as she labored to give birth. [3]Then another sign appeared in the sky; it was a huge red dragon, with seven heads and ten horns, and on its heads were seven diadems. [4]Its tail swept away a third of the stars in the sky and hurled them down to the earth. Then the dragon stood before the woman about to give birth, to devour her child when she gave birth. [5]She gave birth to a son, a male child, destined to rule all the nations with an iron rod. Her child was caught up to God and his throne. [6]The woman herself fled into the desert where she had a place prepared by God, that there she might be taken care of for twelve hundred and sixty days.

The author begins with a series of visions which, unlike the seals and the trumpets, are unnumbered. In this passage, he makes use of ancient mythical images such as those describing Roman, Greek, Persian, and Egyptian gods. Although he does not develop his message according to any single myth, elements from several ancient myths are found in this portion of the Book of Revelation.

The imagery begins with the portrayal of a woman who appears in the sky, clothed with the sun, having the moon under her feet, and wearing a crown of twelve stars. In the Old Testament, we read that God is clothed with the sun (Ps 104) and that the heavenly bodies are controlled by God. The twelve stars point to the twelve signs of the zodiac, but they may also refer to the twelve tribes of Israel. The woman's position in the heavens tells of her power and concern for the people of the earth. The woman, about to give birth, cries aloud because of her labor pains. Although most commentators believe that the birth imagery points to the birth of Jesus, the Messiah, we must be careful not to confuse this woman with Mary. Some early church writers saw this woman as symbolizing the Church, while some later writers applied the imagery both to Mary and to the Church.

A huge, red dragon appears on the scene. The dragon, having seven heads with seven diadems and ten horns, appears in the sky along with the woman. By a mere sweep of his tail, he hurls a third of the stars to the earth. The fallen stars in this vision may refer to the fallen angels. He stands before the woman, ready to devour the child when she gives birth. The story reminds us of the birth of the Greek god Apollo. When Leto, the wife of the god Zeus and the mother of Apollo, was about to give birth to her son, a dragon named Python wanted to kill her. Zeus ordered that Leto be brought to an island for safety where Poseidon, the sea god, protected her by using the sea to keep the island out of the reach of the dragon. A Persian myth also spoke of a three-headed dragon as the symbol of great evil. John apparently adapts these and other myths in shaping his vision.

When the woman gives birth, God acts. The child is Christ, destined to shepherd all nations with the rod of power and he is immediately carried to a share in the glory of God and God's throne. The woman (the Church) flees to a safe, desert place that God has prepared for her. For twelve hundred and sixty days, the limited time given to the power of evil, she will remain in the desert. We as readers should continue to keep in mind that the symbolism of twelve hundred and sixty days—three and a half years—should not be taken literally. This period of time is symbolically intended to evoke the message that evil reigns only for as long as God allows it. The scene is now set for a great battle.

| Rv 12: 7–12 |
|---|

**7Then war broke out in heaven; Michael and his angels battled against the dragon. The dragon and its angels fought back, 8but they did not prevail and there was no longer any place for them in heaven. 9The huge dragon, the ancient serpent, who is called the Devil and Satan, who deceived the whole world, was thrown down to earth, and its angels were thrown down with it.**

**10Then I heard a loud voice in heaven say:**

**"Now have salvation and power come,**

**and the kingdom of our God**

**and the authority of his Anointed.**

**For the accuser of our brothers is cast out,**

**who accuses them before our God day and night.**

**11They conquered him by the blood of the Lamb**

**and by the word of their testimony;**

**love for life did not deter them from death.**

> [12]Therefore, rejoice, you heavens,
>    and you who dwell in them.
> But woe to you, earth and sea,
>    for the Devil has come down to you in great fury,
>    for he knows he has but a short time."

A war breaks out in heaven between the Michael and the dragon and their angels. It was written in the Book of Daniel that a guardian of the people, Michael, would rise up at a time of distress (Dn 12:1). Despite his attempt at fighting Michael and his angels, the dragon and his followers are overwhelmed and cast out of heaven. John identifies the dragon as the ancient serpent, that is, as the tempter in the story of Adam and Eve (Gn 3). John also refers to the dragon as the devil, Satan, the seducer of the world. Although the heavenly conquest of the dragon has taken place, the dragon still possesses power on earth.

John hears a loud voice from heaven that celebrates the victory of God's reign and that of the Anointed One. The "accuser," who continuously and falsely accused the saints before God, was defeated by the death of Christ (the Blood of the Lamb) and the faithfulness of the saints and martyrs. The heavenly rejoicing becomes a warning of woe for the whole earth, since the devil, suffering from a defeat in heaven and aware that the time of his power on earth is limited, will vent his anger on the world.

**Rv 12: 13–18**

[13]When the dragon saw that it had been thrown down to the earth, it pursued the woman who had given birth to the male child. [14]But the woman was given the two wings of the great eagle, so that she could fly to her place in the desert, where, far from the serpent, she was taken care of for a year, two years, and a half-year. [15]The serpent, however, spewed a torrent of water out of his mouth after the woman to sweep her away with the current. [16]But the earth helped the woman and opened its mouth and swallowed the flood that the dragon spewed out of its mouth. [17]Then the dragon became angry with the woman and went off to wage war against the rest of her offspring, those who keep God's commandments and bear witness to Jesus. [18]It took its position on the sand of the sea.

Aware of his heavenly defeat, the dragon now pursues the woman who is the image of the new Israel, the Church. In the Book of Exodus, God tells the people, ". . . I bore you up on eagle's wings" (19:4). John uses the same image here in speaking of the woman who receives the wings of a giant eagle to escape into the desert from the dragon. In the desert, she will be cared for during a period of three and a half years, the period when evil will have power on earth. Just as the People of God were led into the desert to escape the evil power of the pharaoh, so the people of the new Israel are brought to the desert to be protected from the serpent's evil power.

When the serpent discovered that the woman had escaped to the desert, he sent a deluge of water out of his mouth to seek out the woman and carry her off. John pictures the earth as a living person, opening its mouth and swallowing the flood sent by the serpent. This story reflects some of the ancient, mythological stories of the battles between the water gods and the earth gods.

The furious dragon now goes off to war against the offspring of the woman, namely, other members of the Church, who live according to God's commandments and who witness to Jesus. As the passage ends, the dragon takes up his position by the shore of the sea, ready to call forth the first beast.

| | |
|---|---|
| **Rv 13: 1–10** | **13**    *The First Beast*    [1]Then I saw a beast come out of the sea with ten horns and seven heads; on its horns were ten diadems, and on its heads blasphemous name[s]. [2]The beast I saw was like a leopard, but it had feet like a bear's, and its mouth was like the mouth of a lion. To it the dragon gave its own power and throne, along with great authority. [3]I saw that one of its heads seemed to have been mortally wounded, but this mortal wound was healed. Fascinated, the whole world followed after the beast. [4]They worshiped the dragon because it gave its authority to the beast; they also worshiped the beast and said, "Who can compare with the beast or who can fight against it?" |

[5]The beast was given a mouth uttering proud boasts and blasphemies, and it was given authority to act for forty-two months. [6]It opened its mouth to utter blasphemies against God, blaspheming his name and his dwelling and those who dwell in heaven. [7]It was also allowed to wage war against the holy ones and conquer them, and it was granted authority over every tribe, people, tongue, and na-

tion. **⁸All the inhabitants of the earth will worship it, all whose names were not written from the foundation of the world in the book of life, which belongs to the Lamb who was slain.**

　　**⁹Whoever has ears ought to hear these words.**

　　**¹⁰Anyone destined for captivity goes into captivity.**

　　**Anyone destined to be slain by the sword shall be slain by the sword.**

**Such is the faithful endurance of the holy ones.**

The sea was considered by many ancients as the place where evil spirits dwelled. John reports that he saw, coming out of the sea, a beast—with seven heads on which blasphemous names were written and with ten horns containing diadems on each. Commentators believe that this beast, which comes forth from the abode of evil, is a symbol of the chaos inflicted on Christians by the Roman Empire. The seven heads may refer to the seven hills of Rome. The blasphemous names on the heads of the beast may refer to emperor worship and the practice these emperors had of making themselves equal to God.

In the Book of Daniel, the prophet had a dream in which he envisioned four beasts who come forth from the sea (Dn 7:1ff.). John describes the first beast in his vision by putting the characteristics of Daniel's four beasts into his image of the first beast. The beast in John's vision was like a leopard, with paws like a bear, the mouth of a lion, and the great power of the dragon. John already told us that the dragon was Satan, and he now tells us that the dragon gave its power, authority, and throne to the beast (Rome). Thus, the Roman Empire was the beast that stood in the place of Satan on earth.

One of the seven heads of the beast, once mortally wounded, is now healed. Commentators believe that this is a reference to Nero, who was already dead by the time this was written. Some people doubted the first announcement of Nero's death, while others began to believe that he would come back to life to lead an army against Rome. Some people of John's day believed that Nero had fled east to the land of the Parthians and that he would return as the head of the Parthian army and overpower the Roman Empire. Christians, however, saw Nero as the personification of evil, the true Antichrist who would return as a false god to persecute and kill Christians throughout the empire. Some saw Domitian, the ruler of the Roman Empire at the time of John's writing, as the "reborn Nero."

John alludes to emperor worship when he writes that the whole world followed after the beast and worshiped the dragon (Satan) for giving such authority over all nations to the beast. The nations also worshiped the beast through their worship of the Roman emperor and their belief that Rome was too powerful to be overcome. In the Book of Revelation they wonder about who will come forward to conquer the beast. The audience for whom John is writing already knows that Michael had defeated the dragon, the one from whom the beast receives its power.

John tells his readers that the power of the beast was limited to forty-two months (three and a half years). This number continues to be used in the Book of Revelation to symbolize the limitations of the rule of evil in the world. In its power and demand for emperor worship, Rome had become boastful and blasphemous. The Romans not only blasphemed God by demanding emperor worship but they also began to force their blasphemies on God's servants. They began to persecute and kill Christians for refusing to worship the emperor of Rome as a god. Despite all its destructive power, the beast could not act unless it was allowed to do so. God allowed the beast to act in this way, giving it power over the whole world (race, people, language, and nation).

John tells us that all evil people of the world will turn to worship the beast, while the names of those Christians who remain faithful have been written in the book of the living since the world's beginning. John does not intend to give the impression that God has predestined specific people for salvation, but he alludes to the gift of eternal life for those who choose to remain faithful to their Christian commitment. These are the ones who are faithful followers of the Lamb who was slain: they belong to Christ who suffered, died, and was raised. Because of evil's power in the world (allowed by God), Christians can expect to be taken captive and even put to death. Faithfully enduring this hardship and death will be a true sign of God's holy ones on earth.

| Rv 13:<br>11–18 | *The Second Beast* ¹¹Then I saw another beast come up out of the earth; it had two horns like a lamb's but spoke like a dragon. ¹²It wielded all the authority of the first beast in its sight and made the earth and its inhabitants worship the first beast, whose mortal wound had been healed. ¹³It performed great signs, even making fire come down from heaven to earth in the sight of everyone. ¹⁴It deceived the inhabitants of the earth with the signs it was allowed to perform in the sight of the first beast, telling them to make an image for the beast who had been wounded by the sword and revived. ¹⁵It was then permitted to |

breathe life into the beast's image, so that the beast's image could speak and [could] have anyone who did not worship it put to death. [16]It forced all the people, small and great, rich and poor, free and slave, to be given a stamped image on their right hands or their foreheads, [17]so that no one could buy or sell except one who had the stamped image of the beast's name or the number that stood for its name.

[18]Wisdom is needed here; one who understands can calculate the number of the beast, for it is a number that stands for a person. His number is six hundred and sixty-six.

The second beast, which rises up from the earth instead of the sea, has two horns like those of a lamb. This symbol may be pointing to the Antichrist, since Christ is portrayed by John as a lamb. The second beast spoke like a dragon, that is, it spoke the words of evil. This beast makes use of the authority of the first beast in forcing the entire world to worship the first beast, which is Rome. This beast could be a reference to the local authorities within the empire who had their authority from Rome, or it may refer to the cultic priests who forced the people into emperor worship.

In the Book of Kings, Elijah proves that he is a servant of the one true God by having God cast fire down on the earth (1 Kg 18:37–39). This ability to cast fire on the earth was seen as a sign of divine power, and John tells us that the beast will make use of this divine sign. The second beast will have a share in these powers of the first beast, and it will lead many people astray, directing them to make an image of the first beast that was wounded by the sword yet continues to live. This latter image could point to Nero, whose likeness appeared on the Roman coin. Those who refused to offer worship to the emperor, who was recognized as a living god by the local authorities or priests, could be put to death.

John tells us that all people, of every social standing and race, had to accept this mark of the beast on their right hand or forehead. This mark is not a visible mark. Instead, it is a sign of allegiance, much like the sign of the cross is traced today on Christians at the time of their Baptism. Those who did not participate in emperor worship would lose their right to buy and sell the necessities of life.

John now calls on those familiar with the custom of listing a person's name with a number. In the Greek and Hebrew alphabets, the same signs were used for both letters and numbers. John calls for a subtle wisdom when he states that anyone can figure out the number of the beast. The number he gives is six hundred sixty-six, and he states that it points to a specific man. The number six hundred sixty-six is short three times of the number seven. It is less than perfect, and, therefore, the sign of an imperfect person. Some people who preach on the Book of Revelation mistakenly try to apply this number to a person living today, whereas most commentators believe that the numbers add up to the name of Nero.

**Rv 14: 1–5**

**14**    *The Lamb's Companions*    **¹Then I looked and there was the Lamb standing on Mount Zion, and with him a hundred and forty-four thousand who had his name and his Father's name written on their foreheads. ²I heard a sound from heaven like the sound of rushing water or a loud peal of thunder. The sound I heard was like that of harpists playing their harps. ³They were singing [what seemed to be] a new hymn before the throne, before the four living creatures and the elders. No one could learn this hymn except the hundred and forty-four thousand who had been ransomed from the earth. ⁴These are they who were not defiled with women; they are virgins and these are the ones who follow the Lamb wherever he goes. They have been ransomed as the firstfruits of the human race for God and the Lamb. ⁵On their lips no deceit has been found; they are unblemished.**

In the Book of Isaiah, the prophet pictures the Lord as reigning on Mount Zion (24:23). In this next vision, John sees the Lamb standing on Mount Zion, surrounded by the hundred and forty-four thousand people marked with his name and the name of the Father on their foreheads. This hundred and forty-four thousand most likely refers to those mentioned earlier in the Book of Revelation (7:1–8). The scene stands in contrast to the vision of the beast who reigned with those marked with the name of the beast.

John hears sounds from heaven like roaring waters, thunder, and harp music that recall the sounds of God's presence in the Old Testament. He hears a new song which was being sung before the throne, in the presence of the four living creatures and the elders. It was a song that only the hundred and forty-four thousand who were redeemed from the world could learn. These were the ones who have not defiled themselves with women. Such a reference is not to people who have refrained from any sexual relations, but rather to those who have kept themselves pure of any idol worship, which was considered a type of adultery against God. These are the true followers of the Lamb who have been redeemed as the firstfruits for God and the Lamb. The firstfruits of the harvest were those that were consecreted to God. The firstfruits who are the redeemed are those consecrated to God and the Lamb. They are a people without flaw, with nothing deceitful in their lives.

**Rv 14: 6–13**

*The Three Angels*   **⁶Then I saw another angel flying high overhead, with everlasting good news to announce to those who dwell on earth, to every nation, tribe, tongue, and people. ⁷He said in a loud voice, "Fear God and give him glory, for his time has come to sit in judgment. Worship him who made heaven and earth and sea and springs of water."**

**⁸A second angel followed, saying:**

**"Fallen, fallen is Babylon the great,**
**that made all the nations drink**
**the wine of her licentious passion."**

**⁹A third angel followed them and said in a loud voice, "Anyone who worships the beast or its image, or accepts its mark on forehead or hand, ¹⁰will also drink the wine of God's fury, poured full strength into the cup of his wrath, and will be tormented in burning sulfur before the holy angels and before the Lamb. ¹¹The smoke of the fire that torments them will rise forever and ever, and there will be no relief day or night for those who worship the beast or its image or accept the mark of its name." ¹²Here is what sustains the holy ones who keep God's commandments and their faith in Jesus.**

**¹³I heard a voice from heaven say, "Write this: Blessed are the dead who die in the Lord from now on." "Yes," said the Spirit, "let them find rest from their labors, for their works accompany them."**

John sees an angel, the bearer of the eternal good news for all people of the earth. The angel, sharing the news that the time of judgment has arrived, calls all people to give honor and glory to God, the Creator of heaven, earth, the seas, and the springs. The results of this time of judgment are further elaborated in the vision of the next two angels.

John sees a second angel who proclaims that Babylon, who forced all nations to drink her poison, has fallen. Babylon is a symbol for Rome. The words of the angel come from Isaiah who spoke of the fall of Babylon (Is 21:9), and from Jeremiah, who spoke of Babylon making all nations drunk with its wine (51:7).

A third angel warns those who have worshiped the beast or who bear the mark of the beast upon their foreheads or hands that they shall taste the fullness of God's wrath. In the Book of Isaiah, the prophet speaks of God's vengeance on Edom by turning her earth to sulphur and filling her land with eternal smoke (34:8–10). The angel warns those who worship the beast that they will be tormented with burning sulphur in the presence of the angels and before the Lamb and that the smoke of their torment will rise forever, without any relief.

John tells his audience that this news sustains the holy ones who keep God's commands and who remain faithful to Christ by their endurance. John does not intend to paint a picture of the holy ones as rejoicing over the suffering of the wicked, but rather as enduring and strong in their knowledge that evil will be overcome and that they will share in an eternal reward.

A voice from heaven proclaims that those who die in the Lord (those faithful to the Lord) will be blessed because their deeds follow after them.

---

**Rv 14: 14–20**

*The Harvest of the Earth*    [14]Then I looked and there was a white cloud, and sitting on the cloud one who looked like a son of man, with a gold crown on his head and a sharp sickle in his hand. [15]Another angel came out of the temple, crying out in a loud voice to the one sitting on the cloud, "Use your sickle and reap the harvest, for the time to reap has come, because the earth's harvest is fully ripe." [16]So the one who was sitting on the cloud swung his sickle over the earth, and the earth was harvested.

[17]Then another angel came out of the temple in heaven who also had a sharp sickle. [18]Then another angel [came] from the altar, [who] was in charge of the fire, and cried out in a loud voice to the one who had the sharp sickle, "Use your sharp sickle and cut the clusters from the earth's vines, for its grapes are ripe." [19]So the angel swung his sickle over the earth and cut the earth's vintage. He threw it into the great wine press of God's fury. [20]The wine press was trodden outside the city and blood poured out of the wine press to the height of a horse's bridle for two hundred miles.

The next vision recalls an image from the Book of Daniel of "one like the son of man," coming on the clouds of heaven (7:13). John likewise sees one like the son of man, wearing a golden crown and holding a sharpened sickle in his hand, standing on a cloud. The sharpened sickle prepares us for the judgment to follow, while the golden crown symbolizes authority. Some commentators believe that the "one like the son of man" refers to Christ, as it has in an earlier chapter of this book, while others believe that it refers to an angel, because of his apparently subservient role to the command of the angel from heaven who tells him to use his sickle to cut down the harvest. The one on the cloud obeys this call of the angel. John tells us that the angel calls out from the Temple, which is the spiritual temple of heaven, God's throne.

John tells us of another angel who came out of heaven with a sharp sickle. A second angel, the one who cared for the fiery coals before the throne (8:3–5), calls out to the angel with the sickle to gather the harvest from the vines. This other angel throws the gathered grapes into the winepress of God's wrath. In the Book of Isaiah, the prophet, speaking as God, tells of trampling the grapes of God's wrath and crushing the people in this wrath, letting their blood pour out on the ground (63:3–6). Similarly, John describes the blood that poured forth from the winepress in such abundance that it spread like a river for two hundred miles and reached as high as a horse's bridle. This image clearly points to a bloody battle between good and evil.

While some commentators believe that the first image of the "one like the son of man" wielding a sickle and gathering in the wheat refers to Christ as gathering in those who have remained faithful, the majority of commentators are in disagreement. They believe that both images should be taken together as two ways of expressing the same message. In the Book of Joel, the prophet speaks of applying the sickle to the ripe harvest and treading the winepress (4:13). Both images tell of God's wrath and judgment on those who follow the way of evil in the world.

**15**     *The Seven Last Plagues*     **¹Then I saw in heaven another sign, great and awe-inspiring: seven angels with the seven last plagues, for through them God's fury is accomplished.**

Rv 15: 1–4

**²Then I saw something like a sea of glass mingled with fire. On the sea of glass were standing those who had won the victory over the beast and its image and the number that signified its name. They were holding God's harps,**

³and they sang the song of Moses, the servant of God, and
the song of the Lamb:

> "Great and wonderful are your works,
>   Lord God almighty.
> Just and true are your ways,
>   O king of the nations.
> ⁴Who will not fear you, Lord,
>   or glorify your name?
> For you alone are holy.
>   All the nations will come
>   and worship before you,
>   for your righteous acts have been revealed."

John continues his style of moving right into the next series of visions. He
now sees seven angels who are holding the seven final plagues of God's
wrath. In an earlier vision, John had seen a sea of glass that showed God's
position of power both over the earth and over evil spirits who dwelt in the
abode of the sea. Now the saints share in this position of authority,
standing by a calm, glasslike sea that reflects their conquest of evil. This
great sea is mingled with fire, an image of the cleansing fire of the trials
that purify the holy ones. These holy ones have conquered the beast and the
one whose number signified the authority of the beast (the holy ones have
withstood the persecution of the beast and emperor worship).

They hold in their hands the instruments of the heavenly court (harps)
and sing the song of Moses and of the Lamb, praising God and proclaiming
that all nations will come to worship in God's presence as the deeds of God
are clearly recognized. The use of the imagery of the "song of Moses" and
the "song of the Lamb" could be a reference to John's message that the
Lamb now leads the people of God to the new Promised Land as Moses led
God's People to the Promised Land in the Old Testament period.

# Review

1. What message does John reveal in his narrative concerning the woman
   and the dragon?
2. What is the significance of the great battle in heaven between the
   dragon and Michael?
3. What is the message of the first beast?
4. What is the message of the second beast?
5. Who were the companions to the Lamb?
6. What is the message of the three angels?

7. What is the message of the harvest of wheat and grapes?
8. What is the meaning of the final vision of the unnumbered visions?

# For Further Reflection

1. Although the story of the woman and the dragon is not intended to be a prediction for the future, it does have some application to our lives today. What message can we draw from this narrative?
2. The number of the beast is six hundred and sixty-six. Many preachers today try to apply this number to people of our own times, but the Book of Revelation does not intend such an application. Is there any message we can receive for our lives today from this message that points to the number of the beast?

# 6
# The Seven Bowls

Rv 15:
5–8

⁵After this I had another vision. The temple that is the heavenly tent of testimony opened, ⁶and the seven angels with the seven plagues came out of the temple. They were dressed in clean white linen, with a gold sash around their chests. ⁷One of the four living creatures gave the seven angels seven gold bowls filled with the fury of God, who lives forever and ever. ⁸Then the temple became so filled with the smoke from God's glory and might that no one could enter it until the seven plagues of the seven angels had been accomplished.

John has another vision in which he sees the heavenly temple open up, and seven angels, holding the seven plagues, come forth. The angels were clothed in the white linen robes worn by priests who served within the temple and their breasts were circled with golden sashes. One of the four living creatures gives seven bowls filled with the wrath of the eternal God to the seven angels.

When the seven bowls are presented to the seven angels, the heavenly temple is filled with the presence of the power and glory of God, symbolized by smoke so dense that no one could enter heaven. John tells us that no one will be able to enter heaven until the seven plagues of the seven angels come to an end.

Rv 16:
1–11

**16** *The Seven Bowls* ¹I heard a loud voice speaking from the temple to the seven angels, "Go and pour out the seven bowls of God's fury upon the earth."

²The first angel went and poured out his bowl on the earth. Festering and ugly sores broke out on those who had the mark of the beast or worshiped its image.

³The second angel poured out his bowl on the sea. The sea turned to blood like that from a corpse; every creature living in the sea died.

⁴The third angel poured out his bowl on the rivers and springs of water. These also turned to blood. ⁵Then I heard the angel in charge of the waters say:

"You are just, O Holy One,
>    who are and who were,
>    in passing this sentence.
>
> [6]For they have shed the blood of the holy ones and the
>        prophets,
>    and you [have] given them blood to drink;
>    it is what they deserve."
>
> [7]Then I heard the altar cry out,
>    "Yes, Lord God almighty,
>        your judgments are true and just."

[8]The fourth angel poured out his bowl on the sun. It was given the power to burn people with fire. [9]People were burned by the scorching heat and blasphemed the name of God who had power over these plagues, but they did not repent or give him glory.

[10]The fifth angel poured out his bowl on the throne of the beast. Its kingdom was plunged into darkness, and people bit their tongues in pain [11]and blasphemed the God of heaven because of their pains and sores. But they did not repent of their works.

A loud voice calls out from the sanctuary directing the seven angels to pour God's wrath out upon the world. The voice is most likely that of God, since no one is able to approach the temple until the seven plagues come to an end.

In his vision of the plagues, John recalls both the plagues found in the Book of Exodus and the plagues that followed the trumpet blasts mentioned earlier in the Book of Revelation. The first bowl of God's wrath is poured out and it produces boils on those who accepted the mark of the beast or worshiped its image. It reminds the reader of the sixth plague from the Book of Exodus (9:10) when the people of Egypt were afflicted with similar boils.

The second angel pours out his bowl on the earth, and the result is like that of the second trumpet blast (8:10–11) and also the first plague in the Book of Exodus (7:14–25). Just as the Nile is turned to blood, so the sea is turned into the blood of the dead, killing every creature in the sea.

The third angel pours out the third bowl on the rivers and springs, also producing blood. It is reminiscent of the results of the earlier third trumpet blast (8:10–11) and the first plague in the Book of Exodus (7:19). The fresh water becomes poisonous in both plagues. With the third plague comes a proclamation of God as the just and holy One who has given blood to drink to those who shed the blood of the holy ones and the prophets. The altar itself is given a voice and proclaims that God is true and just, a possible reference to the martyrs who were pictured under the altar in an earlier vision. John praised God as the One "who is and who was," since he has now come in these final days. In the first part of his book, God was praised as the One who is, who was, and who is to come.

The fourth bowl is poured out on the sun, causing intense heat that burned the people with fire. These plagues should have led the people to repent, but instead they cursed and blasphemed God.

The fifth bowl is poured out on the throne of the beast, that is, Rome, and the result is like that of the fifth trumpet (9:1–12) and the ninth plague of the Book of Exodus (10:21–23). The kingdom of the beast is cast into darkness and still the people do not repent. They continue to curse and blaspheme God.

**Rv 16: 12–21**

¹²The sixth angel emptied his bowl on the great river Euphrates. Its water was dried up to prepare the way for the kings of the East. ¹³I saw three unclean spirits like frogs come from the mouth of the dragon, from the mouth of the beast, and from the mouth of the false prophet. ¹⁴These were demonic spirits who performed signs. They went out to the kings of the whole world to assemble them for the battle on the great day of God the almighty. ¹⁵("Behold, I am coming like a thief." Blessed is the one who watches and keeps his clothes ready, so that he may not go naked and people see him exposed.) ¹⁶They then assembled the kings in the place that is named Armageddon in Hebrew.

¹⁷The seventh angel poured out his bowl into the air. A loud voice came out of the temple from the throne, saying, "It is done." ¹⁸Then there were lightning flashes, rumblings, and peals of thunder, and a great earthquake. It was such a violent earthquake that there has never been one like it since the human race began on earth. ¹⁹The great city was split into three parts, and the gentile cities fell. But God remembered great Babylon, giving it the cup filled with the wine of his fury and wrath. ²⁰Every island fled, and mountains disappeared. ²¹Large hailstones like

**huge weights came down from the sky on people, and they blasphemed God for the plague of hail because this plague was so severe.**

When the sixth bowl is poured out on the Euphrates River, its waters dry up, opening the way for the kings of the East to attack the Roman Empire. The pouring out of the sixth bowl has a result like that of the sixth trumpet (9:13–21), the plague of the frogs in Exodus (7:25–29) and the parting of the Red Sea (Ex 14:10–22). John sees three unclean spirits, like frogs, coming from the mouth of the dragon, the beast, and the false prophet. They all have powers to perform great signs, thus showing them as images of the Antichrist. They gathered together all the kingdoms of the world in preparation for the great battle.

John warns that this battle will take place suddenly and that everyone should be spiritually clothed so that they do not find themselves naked before the world. He sees this battle as taking place on the final day, the day of the Second Coming of the Lord, and he follows the scriptural theme that this day of judgment will come upon the world suddenly and unexpectedly. The wicked kings will assemble in "Armageddon," the Hebrew name for a place which some have translated to be the Mount of Megiddo. The problem is that there are no mountains in the area of the place called Megiddo, and most commentators admit that the meaning of this symbol remains elusive.

The seventh angel pours his bowl into the empty air, and a loud voice from the throne of heaven proclaims, "It is finished." The apocalyptic images that accompany the Lord's appearance now take place. Lightning, thunder, and earthquakes cover the earth. Unlike the trumpet blasts that had destroyed only a third of the city, the earthquake that accompanies the pouring out of the seventh bowl is the most violent of all earthquakes, splitting the city of Rome into three and destroying all other cities as well. God vents the fullness of his fury against the city of Babylon, that is, against Rome. In the destruction, islands and mountains disappear, and giant hailstones, recalling the seventh plague of Exodus (9:22–26), crush the people. Instead of turning to God and reforming their lives, people curse God for sending the destructive hail.

**Rv 17: 1–6**

**17**    *Babylon the Great*    [1]**Then one of the seven angels who were holding the seven bowls came and said to me, "Come here. I will show you the judgment on the**

great harlot who lives near the many waters. ²The kings of the earth have had intercourse with her, and the inhabitants of the earth became drunk on the wine of her harlotry." ³Then he carried me away in spirit to a deserted place where I saw a woman seated on a scarlet beast that was covered with blasphemous names, with seven heads and ten horns. ⁴The woman was wearing purple and scarlet and adorned with gold, precious stones, and pearls. She held in her hand a gold cup that was filled with the abominable and sordid deeds of her harlotry. ⁵On her forehead was written a name, which is a mystery, "Babylon the great, the mother of harlots and of the abominations of the earth." ⁶I saw that the woman was drunk on the blood of the holy ones and on the blood of the witnesses to Jesus.

As an extension of the message of the seven bowls, one of the angels who held one of the bowls takes John to view the judgment given to the great harlot, seated on many waters. John is speaking here of the Roman Empire. He states that kings of the earth have committed fornication with her and that other nations have grown drunk with her fornication. With these words, John is condemning the nations and people who have followed the idolatrous ways of Rome, accepting its way of life and its false gods. In the Old Testament, the prophets often spoke of the people of God as acting like harlots, lusting after the false gods and the manner of life of other nations (see Ez 16:35–36).

The angel then carries John in spirit to a place of desolation, the place where the evil spirits dwell. He sees a woman who is sitting on a scarlet beast which is completely covered with blasphemous names and has seven heads and ten horns. The scarlet color of the beast may imply royalty, an image that would identify the beast as Roman. The scarlet colors may also refer to blood and fire that have come upon the earth as a result of the ways of the beast. The seven heads refer to the seven hills of Rome, and the ten horns are symbols of the kings who have aligned themselves with Rome. The blasphemous names that cover the beast refer to emperor worship, and the fact that they totally cover the beast shows its total wickedness.

The woman, seated on the beast, is clothed in purple and scarlet and adorned with the jewels of royalty. This description also points to Rome's royalty. The woman holds in her hand a gold cup filled with the sinful and sickening deeds of her fornication. In the Book of Jeremiah, the prophet speaks of Babylon as a golden cup in the hand of the Lord which contaminates the whole world with its contents (Jer 51:7). On the woman's forehead is written an unknown name, apparently a symbol of her dedication to evil. The woman is the new Babylon, Rome, and like the Babylon of old, she is the mother of all those who follow false gods (harlots) and all the disgusting ways of paganism. The woman, Rome, was drunk on the blood of saints and martyrs, that is, she had persecuted and killed many followers of Christ. John tells his readers that he was amazed at the vision of the woman.

**Rv 17: 7–18**

***Meaning of the Beast and Harlot*** When I saw her I was greatly amazed. [7]The angel said to me, "Why are you amazed? I will explain to you the mystery of the woman and of the beast that carries her, the beast with the seven heads and the ten horns. [8]The beast that you saw existed once but now exists no longer. It will come up from the abyss and is headed for destruction. The inhabitants of the earth whose names have not been written in the book of life from the foundation of the world shall be amazed when they see the beast, because it existed once but exists no longer, and yet it will come again. [9]Here is a clue for one who has wisdom. The seven heads represent seven hills upon which the woman sits. They also represent seven kings: [10]five have already fallen, one still lives, and the last has not yet come, and when he comes he must remain only a short while. [11]The beast that existed once but exists no longer is an eighth king, but really belongs to the seven and is headed for destruction. [12]The ten horns that you saw represent ten kings who have not yet been crowned; they will receive royal authority along with the beast for one hour. [13]They are of one mind and will give their power and authority to the beast. [14]They will fight with the Lamb, but the Lamb will conquer them, for he is Lord of lords and king of kings, and those with him are called, chosen, and faithful."

[15]Then he said to me, "The waters that you saw where the harlot lives represent large numbers of peoples, nations, and tongues. [16]The ten horns that you saw and the beast will hate the harlot; they will leave her desolate and

naked; they will eat her flesh and consume her with fire. [17]For God has put it into their minds to carry out his purpose and to make them come to an agreement to give their kingdom to the beast until the words of God are accomplished. [18]The woman whom you saw represents the great city that has sovereignty over the kings of the earth."

Observing John's amazement, the angel interprets for him the meaning behind the woman and the seven-headed beast with the ten horns. The angel tells John the beast had existed once but does not exist anymore. It will come forth again, however, from the abyss before it faces final destruction. John symbolically sees the beast as Nero who lived once, then died, but who, the people believed, will come again. Just as the Lord will come from heaven, so the beast will come from the abyss. The appearance of Nero will bring amazement to all those who have chosen to follow the way of the wicked, those people whose names are not written in the Book of the Living.

The angel continues its interpretation, telling John that the seven heads of the beast symbolize the seven hills on which the woman, who is a symbol of Rome, is enthroned. John tells us that there are seven kings, an apparent reference to the emperors of Rome. The problem, however, is that Rome has had more than seven kings at the time of John's writing. Perhaps he is considering only those kings who caused the most problems for Christians, or those who reigned the longest. He tells us that five have already died, one rules now, and one will follow who will rule for a short period. After that, the one who existed before and who does not exist now will come as the eighth king, although he will have ruled before. This reference continues to point to Nero. The angel foretells that he is already destined for destruction.

The angel explains that the ten horns of the beast are the ten kings who have not yet been crowned. Some commentators believe that these kings represent those who rule certain areas within the empire, while others believe that they represent the Parthian kings. These kings will have power along with the Romans, but the power will be short-lived. After this short period which the author identifies symbolically as "an hour," they will align themselves with the beast (Nero). This follows the legend in which Nero joins forces with the Parthians in the overthrow of Rome. These great armies will fight against the Lamb who will conquer them. The victorious name given to the Lamb is the Lord of Lords and the King of Kings. Those who followed the Lamb will also be victorious.

The angel tells John that the sea on which the woman stands represents the many peoples and nations who came under the power of the woman (Rome). The ten kings (horns) who aligned themselves with the woman will turn on her with hatred and will strip her of her riches, leaving her naked, ravaging her, and setting her on fire. In so doing, they will be carrying out God's plan by joining forces with the beast (Nero) until God's will is complete. Even in the battle among the wicked, the power of God dominates. The angel tells John that the woman is the great city (Rome) that rules over all the kings of the earth.

**Rv 18:
1–8**

**18**    *The Fall of Babylon*    **¹After this I saw another angel coming down from heaven, having great authority, and the earth became illumined by his splendor. ²He cried out in a mighty voice:**

> **"Fallen, fallen is Babylon the great.**
>> **She has become a haunt for demons.**
>
> **She is a cage for every unclean spirit,**
>> **a cage for every unclean bird,**
>> **[a cage for every unclean] and disgusting [beast].**
>
> **³For all the nations have drunk**
>> **the wine of her licentious passion.**
>
> **The kings of the earth had intercourse with her,**
>> **and the merchants of the earth grew rich from her**
>> **drive for luxury."**

**⁴Then I heard another voice from heaven say:**

> **"Depart from her, my people,**
>> **so as not to take part in her sins**
>> **and receive a share in her plagues,**
>
> **⁵for her sins are piled up to the sky,**
>> **and God remembers her crimes.**
>
> **⁶Pay her back as she has paid others.**
>> **Pay her back double for her deeds.**
>> **Into her cup pour double what she poured.**
>
> **⁷To the measure of her boasting and wantonness**
>> **repay her in torment and grief;**
>
> **for she said to herself,**
>> **'I sit enthroned as queen;**
>> **I am no widow,**
>> **and I will never know grief.'**

> [8]Therefore, her plagues will come in one day,
>     pestilence, grief, and famine;
>     she will be consumed by fire.
> For mighty is the Lord God who judges her."

In this vision, John sees another angel (in contrast to the angel in chapter 17) who is pictured as having such an exalted position in God's presence that he lights up the whole world with his glory. The angel cries out with a strong voice that Babylon (Rome), the great, has fallen. John uses many images from the Old Testament, most notably from Isaiah. The words of the angel recall these same words found in the Book of Isaiah concerning the fall of Babylon (Is 21:9). Isaiah later speaks of the land of Edom becoming a wasteland filled with owls and desert ravens (Is 34:11). John speaks of the land of Babylon becoming the haunt of every unclean spirit and hateful bird. In trading with Rome, all nations have become drunk with its wicked ways. The kings have joined hands in sharing in the evils of Rome, and the merchants have grown rich from its evil wealth.

After telling us that Babylon has fallen, the scene seems to move back to the time just before the fall. Another voice from heaven urges God's people to leave the city lest in sharing in its sinfulness, they will also share in its disaster. God intends to punish the city, giving it the afflictions it has given to others, and giving doublefold. In the Book of Isaiah, the prophet spoke of Babylon as bragging like a sovereign mistress who will never lose those things to which she has attached herself. She will never be a widow. Isaiah warns that she will lose all in a single day (Is 47:7–9). John pictures his Babylon (Rome) in the same way, seeing her as bragging that she is a queen who will never become a widow. Like Isaiah, John foretells that every kind of death and disaster will suddenly come upon her. Besides death, mourning, and famine, the mighty Lord and God will destroy her with a judgment of fire.

**Rv 18: 9–24**

> [9]The kings of the earth who had intercourse with her in their wantonness will weep and mourn over her when they see the smoke of her pyre. [10]They will keep their distance for fear of the torment inflicted on her, and they will say:
>
>> "Alas, alas, great city,
>>     Babylon, mighty city.
>>     In one hour your judgment has come."

[11]The merchants of the earth will weep and mourn for her, because there will be no more markets for their cargo: [12]their cargo of gold, silver, precious stones, and pearls; fine linen, purple silk, and scarlet cloth; fragrant wood of every kind, all articles of ivory and all articles of the most expensive wood, bronze, iron, and marble; [13]cinnamon, spice, incense, myrrh, and frankincense; wine, olive oil, fine flour, and wheat; cattle and sheep, horses and chariots, and slaves, that is, human beings.

[14]"The fruit you craved
    has left you.
All your luxury and splendor are gone,
    never again will one find them."

[15]The merchants who deal in these goods, who grew rich from her, will keep their distance for fear of the torment inflicted on her. Weeping and mourning, [16]they cry out:

"Alas, alas, great city,
    wearing fine linen, purple and scarlet,
    adorned [in] gold, precious stones, and pearls.
[17]In one hour this great wealth has been ruined."

Every captain of a ship, every traveler at sea, sailors, and seafaring merchants stood at a distance [18]and cried out when they saw the smoke of her pyre, "What city could compare with the great city?" [19]They threw dust on their heads and cried out, weeping and mourning:

"Alas, alas, great city,
    in which all who had ships at sea
    grew rich from her wealth.
In one hour she has been ruined.
[20]Rejoice over her, heaven,
    you holy ones, apostles, and prophets.
For God has judged your case against her."

[21]A mighty angel picked up a stone like a huge millstone and threw it into the sea and said:

"With such force will Babylon the great city be thrown
        down,
    and will never be found again.
[22]No melodies of harpists and musicians,
    flutists and trumpeters,
    will ever be heard in you again.

No craftsmen in any trade
will ever be found in you again.
No sound of the millstone
will ever be heard in you again.
[23]No light from a lamp
will ever be seen in you again.
No voices of bride and groom
will ever be heard in you again.
Because your merchants were the great ones of the
world,
all nations were led astray by your magic potion.
[24]In her was found the blood of prophets and holy ones
and all who have been slain on the earth."

The Book of Ezekiel speaks of the rulers leaving their thrones and stripping themselves of all ornaments to mourn the destruction of Tyre (26:16). Ezekiel also tells of the mariners lamenting the loss of their trade with Tyre in its destruction (27:28–36). These images now appear in John's description of the reaction of the kings, merchants, and seamen to the destruction of Rome. The kings of the earth who joined with Rome to perform wicked deeds will mourn and lament when they see the smoke, rising as a sign of her destruction. They will bewail that the great city of Babylon (Rome) has met its destruction in a single hour.

The merchants will weep and mourn because they no longer have anyone to purchase their goods. John lists the rich and luxurious items involved in the merchant's trade. Most of these items are named in the Book of Ezekiel (27:9–25). The items of wealth mentioned here show not only the luxury Rome sought from these merchants but also the role of the merchants in all the wicked deeds of Rome, including the selling of slaves. Those goods Rome craved were not sought after when Rome was destroyed. Just as the kings kept a distance to bewail their loss, so the merchants do the same, wailing in the same way as the kings. They cry out that the great city—in its fine clothing and ornamentation—has had its wealth destroyed in a single hour.

Those who made their living on the sea look at the destruction of Rome and also join in bewailing the loss of the great city. They ask what other city could compare with the greatness of Rome. They go into mourning, pouring dust on their heads and crying out that the great city which made them rich from her trade has been destroyed in a single hour. The tone of the writing suddenly changes as the angel calls all of heaven—

the saints, the apostles, and the prophets—to rejoice since God has now brought the deserved punishment on the great city.

John continues to make use of Old Testament images as he speaks of a mighty angel hurling a stone as great as a millstone into the sea. In the Book of Jeremiah, the prophet spoke of a book being thrown into the river and sinking as Babylon will sink (52:25). When the angel hurls the stone into the sea, it is meant to be an image of the great fall of the Babylon of John's day—Rome. Like Jeremiah's Babylon, the great city will be cast down with violence and will completely disappear. The sound of its music, its craftsmen, and the grinding of the mill shall be heard no more. No light will shine from it, and no bride and groom will be found in it. The daily routine of its life will exist no longer. Those who traded with Rome were considered the wealthy people of the day, and many were led astray by its wicked allurements. Central to these allurements was emperor worship.

**Rv 19: 1–10**

**19** ¹After this I heard what sounded like the loud voice of a great multitude in heaven, saying:

"Alleluia!

Salvation, glory, and might belong to our God,

²for true and just are his judgments.

He has condemned the great harlot

who corrupted the earth with her harlotry.

He has avenged on her the blood of his servants."

³They said a second time:

"Alleluia! Smoke will rise from her forever and ever."

⁴The twenty-four elders and the four living creatures fell down and worshiped God who sat on the throne, saying, "Amen. Alleluia."

*The Victory Song*    ⁵A voice coming from the throne said:

"Praise our God, all you his servants,

[and] you who revere him, small and great."

⁶Then I heard something like the sound of a great multitude or the sound of rushing water or mighty peals of thunder, as they said:

"Alleluia!

The Lord has established his reign,

[our] God, the almighty.

⁷Let us rejoice and be glad

and give him glory.

For the wedding day of the Lamb has come,
  his bride has made herself ready.
⁸She was allowed to wear
  a bright, clean linen garment."
(The linen represents the righteous deeds of the holy ones.)
⁹Then the angel said to me, "Write this: Blessed are those who have been called to the wedding feast of the Lamb." And he said to me, "These words are true; they come from God." ¹⁰I fell at his feet to worship him. But he said to me, "Don't! I am a fellow servant of yours and of your brothers who bear witness to Jesus. Worship God. Witness to Jesus is the spirit of prophecy."

Now a festive atmosphere fills the heavens as a multitude of voices sing a song of praise to God's victory. The multitude begins with its "Alleluia" proclamation. Much more than a simple expression of joy, this proclamation is a prayer of praise for God. The voices praise God, the true and just Judge for condemning the harlot (Rome) who contaminated the world. The heavenly voices rejoice in the vengeance that God has taken on those who persecuted the holy ones. This rejoicing over God's vengeance, as that in the past, does not take pleasure in seeing others suffer but instead rejoices that God has acted with justice and has shown the eventual victory of good over evil.

Another cry of "Alleluia" is heard as the smoke continues to rise from the city. The four elders in the heavenly court again fall down before God, who is seated on the throne. They proclaim their agreement and praise with "Amen! Alleluia!" A voice from the throne calls all God's servants—great and small—to praise God. A resounding response—like a large crowd, a roaring torrent, or thunder—proclaim a "Alleluia" to the Lord, the King, who is the all-powerful God. The voices rejoice because the wedding day of the Lamb has come, the day when the Lord joins with all the faithful for all eternity. The wedding dress is made of white linen, representing the good deeds of all the saints.

The angel tells John to write that those chosen to share in the wedding feast of the Lamb are blessed. This beatitude recalls the Jewish image of the messianic age, which was often pictured as a banquet. The angel tells John that these words, which come from God, are true. John falls to the ground to worship the angel, but the angel resists this worship, telling John that he is only a servant as John and the other saints are. God alone is worthy of such worship. John may have placed this message here to offset a growing tendency toward angel worship in some early Church communities. The true spirit of witnessing shows itself in those who witness to Christ.

# Review

1. What is the meaning of the first four bowls poured out by the four angels?
2. What is the meaning of the last three bowls which were poured out by the last three angels?
3. What vision of Babylon and the beast does John have, and what interpretation does the angel give to this vision?
4. What destruction does the angel see in the fall of Babylon, and what warning is given to the saints?
5. What is the reaction of the kings, the merchants, and the mariners to the destruction of Babylon?
6. Why is there rejoicing in heaven over the destruction of Babylon?
7. What are some elements of the prayer of rejoicing at the fall of Babylon?

# For Further Reflection

1. John speaks of the effect of the destruction of Babylon (Rome) on the people of his own day. Do we have any Babylons today, and what would happen if they were destroyed?
2. The reason given for rejoicing over the destruction of Babylon is not a hateful revenge, but a joyful response to the power and victory of good over evil. Do we feel that God should take vengeance on the world today, and, if so, why do we feel this way?

# 7
# Fulfilling God's Plan

Rv 19:
11–16

**The King of Kings** <sup>11</sup>**Then I saw the heavens opened, and there was a white horse; its rider was [called] "Faithful and True." He judges and wages war in righteousness. <sup>12</sup>His eyes were [like] a fiery flame, and on his head were many diadems. He had a name inscribed that no one knows except himself. <sup>13</sup>He wore a cloak that had been dipped in blood, and his name was called the Word of God. <sup>14</sup>The armies of heaven followed him, mounted on white horses and wearing clean white linen. <sup>15</sup>Out of his mouth came a sharp sword to strike the nations. He will rule them with an iron rod, and he himself will tread out in the wine press the wine of the fury and wrath of God the almighty. <sup>16</sup>He has a name written on his cloak and on his thigh, "King of kings and Lord of lords."**

This passage brings together many images of Christ found in the early chapters of the Book of Revelation. John sees the heavens open, and a white horse appears with a rider whose name is "Faithful and True." In the letter to Laodicea (3:14), the one who sends the message (Christ) is referred to as the faithful and true witness. In the letters to the seven churches (1:9–3:22), Christ is portrayed as the one who judges the churches. In the present passage, John describes Christ as the one who acts with justice in judging and making war on God's enemies. He has eyes like flames of fire which see all. In the opening chapters of the Book of Revelation (1:14, 2:18), Christ is pictured as having eyes like fire. Just as the beast, Christ is pictured as having many diadems on his head, showing his authority over the beast.

John tells us that Christ has a name inscribed on him that only Christ knows. Here John may be following the semetic attitude toward knowing one's name: to know a person's true name was to know everything about that person. Since no one (except God) could know Christ fully, then no one could know his name. John tells us that he wore a cloak dipped in the blood of his enemies. After telling us that no one knows his name, John tells us that his name is the Word of God. This may be a reference to the name of the Son of God identified in John's Gospel where he is called the

Word, or it may refer to that which Christ does, namely, that he spreads the Word of God. Armies from heaven, riding white horses and dressed in fine linen, come behind Christ. The white horses and fine linen identified the members of these armies as the saints who were described earlier as clothed in white garments.

A sharp sword for striking down the nations—that is, for judging them—comes out of his mouth. This recalls the two-edged sword that came from the mouth of Christ, as described in the opening lines of Revelation (1:18). He will shepherd with an iron rod and will tread the winepress of God's wrath. The Book of Isaiah speaks of God treading out the winepress and becoming red with the blood of the people (63:1–6). This treading of the winepress was described earlier in the Book of Revelation (14:6, 17:6). Just as the beast was covered with blasphemous names, the robe worn by Christ on his thigh is covered with a name that identifies him as the King of Kings and the Lord of Lords.

| Rv 19: 17–21 | [17]Then I saw an angel standing on the sun. He cried out [in] a loud voice to all the birds flying high overhead, "Come here. Gather for God's great feast, [18]to eat the flesh of kings, the flesh of military officers, and the flesh of warriors, the flesh of horses and of their riders, and the flesh of all, free and slave, small and great." [19]Then I saw the beast and the kings of the earth and their armies gathered to fight against the one riding the horse and against his army. [20]The beast was caught and with it the false prophet who had performed in its sight the signs by which he led astray those who had accepted the mark of the beast and those who had worshiped its image. The two were thrown alive into the fiery pool burning with sulfur. [21]The rest were killed by the sword that came out of the mouth of the one riding the horse, and all the birds gorged themselves on their flesh. |
|---|---|

John sees an angel, described as standing in the sun, who calls all carrion birds in midheaven to come and gather for the great feast God has prepared for them. They are to eat the flesh of kings, captains, warriors, horses and their riders, the free and the slaves, the great and the small. In the Book of Ezekiel, the prophet was told to prophesy against Gog, an evil prince who wars against Israel (39:1–5). The prophet warned Gog that his army will be eaten by birds of prey. Later in the same chapter, the Lord told the prophet to call together every kind of bird and to tell them to gather for the slaughter, promising that they will have an abundance of flesh to eat and blood to drink (Ez 39:17–20). Utilizing this prophecy from Ezekiel, John speaks of the great battle that is about to take place.

John does not speak of the battle, but rather of its results. He tells of the battlelines drawn up between the armies of the beast and the kings and the army of the One riding the white horse. John next tells us that both the beast and the false prophet are captured. The false prophet, described as performing great signs that led the people to accept the mark of the beast and to worship its image, is the second beast mentioned earlier in Revelation (13:11–17). The beast and the false prophet are cast down into the burning pit of damnation, while the rest were slain by the sword that came out of the mouth of the one who rode the horse, Christ and his army. The birds have a gluttonous feast upon the flesh of the dead.

**Rv 20: 1–10**

**20**    *The Thousand-year Reign*    **¹Then I saw an angel come down from heaven, holding in his hand the key to the abyss and a heavy chain. ²He seized the dragon, the ancient serpent, which is the Devil or Satan, and tied it up for a thousand years ³and threw it into the abyss, which he locked over it and sealed, so that it could no longer lead the nations astray until the thousand years are completed. After this, it is to be released for a short time.**

**⁴Then I saw thrones; those who sat on them were entrusted with judgment. I also saw the souls of those who had been beheaded for their witness to Jesus and for the word of God, and who had not worshiped the beast or its image nor had accepted its mark on their foreheads or hands. They came to life and they reigned with Christ for a thousand years. ⁵The rest of the dead did not come to life until the thousand years were over. This is the first resurrection. ⁶Blessed and holy is the one who shares in the first resurrection. The second death has no power over these; they will be priests of God and of Christ, and they will reign with him for [the] thousand years.**

**⁷When the thousand years are completed, Satan will be released from his prison. ⁸He will go out to deceive the nations at the four corners of the earth, Gog and Magog, to gather them for battle; their number is like the sand of the**

sea. ⁹They invaded the breadth of the earth and surrounded the camp of the holy ones and the beloved city. But fire came down from heaven and consumed them. ¹⁰The Devil who had led them astray was thrown into the pool of fire and sulfur, where the beast and the false prophet were. There they will be tormented day and night forever and ever.

In an earlier chapter of the Book of Revelation (9:1–11), John tells his readers of the fifth trumpet blast that leads to an angel coming from heaven and opening the great abyss. Now he sees an angel come down from heaven with the key to the abyss and a great chain in his hand. The angel chains the dragon, which he calls the ancient serpent, the devil or Satan, and he seals him in the abyss. The dragon is chained for a thousand years. The thousand years is a symbolic number of years representing a long, indefinite period of time. During this time period, the dragon will not be able to lead any nations astray; but after this period is ended, the dragon will be released for a short while.

During this thousand-year period, John sees a time when goodness reigns and where thrones are set up for those who remained faithful. They receive the power to pass judgment, although John does not tell us whom they are to judge. He also sees the spirits of those who had been beheaded for their witness to Christ and for refusing to worship the beast or accept its mark. These are the martyrs who remained faithful. John tells us that they have risen from the dead and that they now reign with Christ for a thousand years. Others, good as well as bad, would not rise until the thousand years had ended. Those who share in this first resurrection will not undergo a second death. They are the holy and blessed ones who are the priests of God and Christ and who reign for the thousand years.

At the end of the thousand years (the indefinite period of time), Satan will be released and will deceive all the nations at the four corners of the world. In the Book of Ezekiel, the prophet spoke of Gog who enters battle against the people of Israel (38–40). Gog comes from a land called Magog. John speaks of Satan as gathering the countless array of troops from Gog and Magog for battle against God's people. When they surround the country and the city where God's people are located, fire came down from heaven and devoured them. The fire from heaven implies that God has now entered into the battle. The devil is cast into the lake of fire where the beast and the false prophet were thrown earlier. All three now face eternal torment.

Rv 20:
11–15

*The Large White Throne*    ¹¹Next I saw a large white throne and the one who was sitting on it. The earth and the sky fled from his presence and there was no place for them. ¹²I saw the dead, the great and the lowly, standing before the throne, and scrolls were opened. Then another scroll was opened, the book of life. The dead were judged according to their deeds, by what was written in the scrolls. ¹³The sea gave up its dead; then Death and Hades gave up their dead. All the dead were judged according to their deeds. ¹⁴Then Death and Hades were thrown into the pool of fire. (This pool of fire is the second death.) ¹⁵Anyone whose name was not found written in the book of life was thrown into the pool of fire.

John sees a large white throne of judgment. The One who sits on it is God, the Judge. John describes the end of the world by stating that the earth and the sky fled from God's presence until they could be seen no more. He pictures the general judgment where all the dead—the great and the lowly—stand before God's throne. The Book of the Living—the book containing the names of all those who remained faithful—is opened and the dead are judged according to their deeds. The sea, the abode of chaos and evil, gives up its dead as does death and the abode of the dead. Death and the abode of the dead are treated as if they are living beings and are cast into the pit of fire, the final and second death, which is eternal. Those whose names were not found in the Book of the Living share the same fate by being thrown with them into the pit of fire.

Rv 21:
1–8

**21**    *The New Heaven and the New Earth*    ¹Then I saw a new heaven and a new earth. The former heaven and the former earth had passed away, and the sea was no more. ²I also saw the holy city, a new Jerusalem, coming down out of heaven from God, prepared as a bride adorned for her husband. ³I heard a loud voice from the throne saying, "Behold, God's dwelling is with the human race. He will dwell with them and they will be his people and God himself will always be with them [as their God]. ⁴He will wipe every tear from their eyes, and there shall be no more death or mourning, wailing or pain, [for] the old order has passed away."

⁵The one who sat on the throne said, "Behold, I make all things new." Then he said, "Write these words down,

for they are trustworthy and true." [6]He said to me, "They are accomplished. I [am] the Alpha and the Omega, the beginning and the end. To the thirsty I will give a gift from the spring of life-giving water. [7]The victor will inherit these gifts, and I shall be his God, and he will be my son. [8]But as for cowards, the unfaithful, the depraved, murderers, the unchaste, sorcerers, idol-worshipers, and deceivers of every sort, their lot is in the burning pool of fire and sulfur, which is the second death."

Isaiah had God speak of creating a new heaven and a new earth in which the past would no longer be remembered (Is 65:17). John begins this chapter with a vision of the new heavens and the new earth. The previous heaven and earth had passed away, and the sea had passed away with it. The sea was the abode of evil and chaos, and John states that there is no room for them in this new heaven and new earth.

John next sees the new Jerusalem, the holy city that comes from heaven like a bride prepared to meet her husband. This holy city, called the new Jerusalem, has no connection with the real city of Jerusalem. It is the eternal dwelling place of the Church and those who remained faithful to Christ. Jerusalem is pictured as a bride ready to be espoused to the Lamb. A great voice from heaven proclaims that this new city is God's dwelling place among the people. This new dwelling place for God was expected as far back as Ezekiel (37:26–28). God will be with the people, and all the imperfections and tragedies of our present existence will no longer exist. We will no longer weep or experience pain.

The One who sits on the throne announces that he makes all things new. God is the Alpha and the Omega, the beginning and the end (see 1:8). God will satisfy all who thirst with the life-giving waters. Those who remain faithful will be the true conquerors who will receive the gift of having the true God as their God and will be called Children of God. Those who rejected the faith and practiced evil deeds will be cast into the pool of fire and will share in the second, eternal death.

*The New Jerusalem*    Rv 21: 9–27    [9]One of the seven angels who held the seven bowls filled with the seven last plagues came and said to me, "Come here. I will show you the bride, the wife of the Lamb." [10]He took me in spirit to a great, high mountain and showed me the holy city Jerusalem coming down out of heaven from God. [11]It gleamed with the splendor of God. Its radiance was like that of a precious stone, like jasper, clear as crystal. [12]It had a massive, high wall, with twelve gates where twelve angels were stationed and on which names were inscribed, [the names] of the twelve tribes of the Israelites. [13]There were three gates facing east, three north, three south, and three west. [14]The wall of the city had twelve courses of stones as its foundation, on which were inscribed the twelve names of the twelve apostles of the Lamb.

[15]The one who spoke to me held a gold measuring rod to measure the city, its gates, and its wall. [16]The city was square, its length the same as [also] its width. He measured the city with the rod and found it fifteen hundred miles in length and width and height. [17]He also measured its wall: one hundred and forty-four cubits according to the standard unit of measurement the angel used. [18]The wall was constructed of jasper, while the city was pure gold, clear as glass. [19]The foundations of the city wall were decorated with every precious stone; the first course of stones was jasper, the second sapphire, the third chalcedony, the fourth emerald, [20]the fifth sardonyx, the sixth carnelian, the seventh chrysolite, the eighth beryl, the ninth topaz, the tenth chrysoprase, the eleventh hyacinth, and the twelfth amethyst. [21]The twelve gates were twelve pearls, each of the gates made from a single pearl; and the street of the city was of pure gold, transparent as glass.

[22]I saw no temple in the city, for its temple is the Lord God almighty and the Lamb. [23]The city had no need of sun or moon to shine on it, for the glory of God gave it light, and its lamp was the Lamb. [24]The nations will walk by its light, and to it the kings of the earth will bring their treasure. [25]During the day its gates will never be shut, and there will be no night there. [26]The treasure and wealth of the nations will be brought there, [27]but nothing unclean will enter it, nor any[one] who does abominable things or tells lies. Only those will enter whose names are written in the Lamb's book of life.

In chapter 17 of the Book of Revelation, one of the angels with the seven bowls took John to witness the judgment in store for the harlot of Babylon (17:1). In this chapter, one of the seven angels with the seven bowls filled with the seven last plagues takes John to witness the woman who is the bride of the Lamb. In this way, the bride of the Lamb is contrasted with the harlot of Babylon. Much of the imagery found in this chapter comes from the Book of Ezekiel. Just as Ezekiel was brought in a divine vision to a high mountain where he saw a city being built (40:1–2), so John is now brought in spirit to a high mountain where he sees the city of Jerusalem coming down from heaven. This is not the city of Jerusalem on earth, but a symbolic new and holy dwelling place for God's faithful.

In the Book of Ezekiel, the Temple is measured and described from all angles (40:1ff.). John describes the heavenly Jerusalem as glowing with the glory of God and possessing the radiance of a rare jewel, sparkling like a precious diamond. The walls were high and had three gates on each side, twelve gates in all. On the gates were written the names of the twelve tribes of Israel. This reference is not meant to imply that only the physical descendants of the twelve tribes had a part in the city, but that it was a spiritual city for those who lived in the spirit of God's people. The city had twelve foundations on which were written the twelve names of the Apostles of the Lamb. This imagery shows that the Apostles of the Lamb (Christ) also shared in the foundation of this great city. Just as Ezekiel saw a man measuring the new city with his measuring rod (Ez 40:3ff.), so John sees the angel who was speaking to him measuring the city with a measuring rod of gold. The city was a perfect cube, twelve thousand stadia (approximately 1,500 miles to a stadia) in length, width, and height. The wall of the city, composed of rare and precious jewels from its foundation to its peak, measured one hundred and forty-four cubits in height (approximately 216 feet). The one hundred and forty-four cubits should be taken symbolically to refer to the twelve tribes of Israel multiplied by the twelve Apostles of the Lamb, all of whom are called to share in this heavenly new Jerusalem. The twelve gates of the city were each composed of a single pearl, and the streets were made of gold and were transparent as glass.

Unlike the vision found in Ezekiel, the city had no Temple within it, since the Lord God Almighty and the Lamb filled the city and were themselves the living temple. The glory of God and the Lamb was so magnificent that the city needed neither sun nor moon. In the Book of Isaiah, the prophet told of the glory of the new Zion that lives in the light of the Lord's glory (60:1–4). Isaiah further states that all nations will walk by this light and that kings will walk in its radiance. John borrows this imagery to speak of the new Jerusalem, telling his readers that nations will walk by the light of this new Jerusalem and that kings shall bring their treasures to it. In a later verse of the same chapter, Isaiah writes that the gates of Zion will never be closed (Is 60:11). John states that the gates of the new Jerusalem will never be closed during the day, which signifies they will always be open since the radiance of God never ends, and, as a result, there is no night in this city. This heavenly Jerusalem will receive the treasures and riches of the nations, but no profane person or thing will enter it. Only those whose names are written in the Book of the Living, as kept by the Lamb, will be permitted to enter this city.

**Rv 22: 1–5**

**22   ¹Then the angel showed me the river of life-giving water, sparkling like crystal, flowing from the throne of God and of the Lamb ²down the middle of its street. On either side of the river grew the tree of life that produces fruit twelve times a year, once each month; the leaves of the trees serve as medicine for the nations. ³Nothing accursed will be found there anymore. The throne of God and of the Lamb will be in it, and his servants will worship him. ⁴They will look upon his face, and his name will be on their foreheads. ⁵Night will be no more, nor will they need light from lamp or sun, for the Lord God shall give them light, and they shall reign forever and ever.**

In the Book of Ezekiel, the prophet speaks of water flowing out of the sanctuary. Fruit trees grew along its banks, providing fresh fruit each month and a source of healing from its leaves (47:12). An angel shows John a river of life-giving water that flowed from the throne of God and from the Lamb. As it flowed down the middle of the street of the city, it nourished the trees of life along its banks. These trees of life recall the tree of life found in the Book of Genesis (2:9–10), but John's imagery is closer to that found in the Book of Ezekiel. These trees produced fruit twelve times a year—once each month—and their leaves provided healing for the nations. Nothing shall be cursed in this city where the throne of God and the Lamb reside and where God's servants offer worship. In the Book of Exodus, Moses was not allowed to see God's face, since anyone who looked at it could not continue to live (33:20). John tells us that the people of the heavenly Jerusalem will see God face to face and will bear the intimate name of God on their foreheads. They will no longer experience the darkness of night, and will have no further need for lamps or the sun: The glory of the Lord God will provide light for them, and they shall live in this heavenly city forever.

Rv 22:
6–21

[6]And he said to me, "These words are trustworthy and true, and the Lord, the God of prophetic spirits, sent his angel to show his servants what must happen soon."

[7]"Behold, I am coming soon." Blessed is the one who keeps the prophetic message of this book.

[8]It is I, John, who heard and saw these things, and when I heard and saw them I fell down to worship at the feet of the angel who showed them to me. [9]But he said to me, "Don't! I am a fellow servant of yours and of your brothers the prophets and of those who keep the message of this book. Worship God."

[10]Then he said to me, "Do not seal up the prophetic words of this book, for the appointed time is near. [11]Let the wicked still act wickedly, and the filthy still be filthy. The righteous must still do right, and the holy still be holy."

[12]"Behold, I am coming soon. I bring with me the recompense I will give to each according to his deeds. [13]I am the Alpha and the Omega, the first and the last, the beginning and the end."

[14]Blessed are they who wash their robes so as to have the right to the tree of life and enter the city through its gates. [15]Outside are the dogs, the sorcerers, the unchaste, the murderers, the idol-worshipers, and all who love and practice deceit.

[16]"I, Jesus, sent my angel to give you this testimony for the churches. I am the root and offspring of David, the bright morning star."

[17]The Spirit and the bride say, "Come." Let the hearer say, "Come." Let the one who thirsts come forward, and the one who wants it receive the gift of life-giving water.

[18]I warn everyone who hears the prophetic words in this book: if anyone adds to them, God will add to him the plagues described in this book, [19]and if anyone takes away from the words in this prophetic book, God will take away his share in the tree of life and in the holy city described in this book.

[20]The one who gives this testimony says, "Yes, I am coming soon." Amen! Come, Lord Jesus!

[21]The grace of the Lord Jesus be with all.

Most commentators view these last verses as a type of epilogue to the Book of Revelation based on the belief that the official apocalyptic message ended with the previous passage about the heavenly Jerusalem. An angel—who may likely have been the same angel who brought John the vision of the heavenly Jerusalem—now speaks to John. Christ is named "Faithful and True" in an earlier chapter (19:11). The angel now tells John that these words from Christ are faithful and true. The angel is sent by the Lord, the God of all prophetic spirits, to bring this message to the servants of God and the Lamb. Apocalyptic writings concern those things predicted to occur soon, and the angel asserts that these words concern those things which are to happen soon.

In the midst of the angel's message, Christ himself begins to speak (as he will do several times in the epilogue). He calls his hearers to remember that he is coming soon, and he repeats a beatitude found in the opening lines of Revelation (1:3) and blesses those who listen to the message of this book and put it into action.

John tells his audience (as he has done at the opening of the book) that he is the one who heard and saw the events disclosed in this book. When he did so, he fell down to worship an angel and was warned that he should worship God alone, not an angel who is merely a servant along with John, the prophets, and those who live the message found in this book. John had earlier been warned (19:10) that he should not worship the angel.

In the Book of Daniel, the prophet was told to keep the message secret and to seal the book until the end of time (12:4). In contrast to the directive given to Daniel, John is told not to seal up the book, since the appointed time (the end time) is near. The wicked will continue in their wicked ways, and the virtuous will continue in the ways of virtue and holiness.

Christ again speaks, reminding his listeners that he is coming soon to share the just rewards according to the deeds of each person. He declares that he is the Alpha and Omega, the First and the Last, the Beginning and the End. With the coming of Christ, the End is near. Those who have washed their robes (remained faithful in the Blood of the Lamb) will have a right to the tree of life and will enter through the gates of the city. Those outside are the ones who have practiced every type of wickedness.

Christ again speaks as the One who has sent the angels to the churches, calling himself the root and offspring of David, the Morning Star. These are all messianic images found in the Old Testament. The Spirit and the Bride (the Church) bids all who thirst to come and share in the life-giving waters.

John ends with the typical apocalyptic warning. He offers himself as a witness to this message, warning that anyone who adds to the message will be punished with the plagues found in this book and that those who take anything away from this message will not share in the tree of life and the heavenly city.

John tells us that the one who gives the testimony found in this book proclaims that he is coming soon. John's response is one of loving agreement: "Amen! Come Lord Jesus!" This prayer, "Come Lord Jesus," was a liturgical prayer used in the early Church.

The Book of Revelation concludes with the typical ending for a letter. John wishes his audience the grace of the Lord Jesus, which seems to point to the idea that the book, like a letter, is to be read by all.

# Review

1. How does John describe the King of kings and Lord of lords who comes from heaven?
2. What is the meaning behind the birds of prey and their great feast on the flesh of the slain?
3. What will happen during the thousand-year reign?
4. What does John tell us about the new heaven and new earth?
5. What is the meaning behind the river that nourishes fruit trees bearing leaves that heal and new fruit each month?
6. Why is John told not to seal up the message of his book?
7. What is the significance of the invitation, "Come, Lord Jesus"?

# For Further Reflection

1. A major question from many people concerns the mystery of suffering in life. Why does God allow people to suffer? If you were to use the Book of Revelation to answer this question, what answer would you give?
2. John talks about a new heaven and a new earth as an image of eternal happiness for the faithful. What message about eternal life is provided in this passage?

# Conclusion

Since we live at a time when science fiction is so popular, we often allow our imaginations to carry us into a world of the future that no longer seems improbable. We see ordinary people traveling from one planet to another, and we see great wars being fought with beams rather than bullets or bombs. We are living in an age when scientific discovery is moving so quickly that nothing seems impossible. Science fiction, therefore, has the ability to link the present with the future.

Let us imagine one planet in the future on which there is a large parking lot of rocket ships. The people are all gathered in a giant stadium, and a speaker is standing on a platform in the center, waving a Bible as he speaks. By this time in history, scientists have discovered how to build large stadiums in such a way that the voice of the speaker carries to all parts of the stadium without a microphone.

He shouts out to the audience, "The other day, as I was traveling throughout the galaxy, I saw some stars falling from the sky and others were breaking up in giant earthquakes. We now have battles between the planets. There are rumors that more people will be killed, so many that the birds of prey will have to eat them because we cannot possibly bury them. Read Revelation and know that these are signs of the end of the world. We must repent because the Bible is telling us that the end is near."

As strange as this picture might be to us today, it does point out a fact of history. Many preachers down through history have given a literal interpretation to the Book of Revelation, and in so doing have been able to sway people—through fear—to turn to God. Every century has had its preachers of doom, and most of them have made their predictions based on their intepretations of the Book of Revelation. In doing so, they have missed the great message of the book, namely, that evil can act in the world only because God allows it, and only as long as God allows it. Those who must suffer during this period will share in the victory of the new heaven and the new earth. Revelation is a book of hope in the midst of turmoil, not a book of doom.

*Notes*

# Notes